Total Quality Management (TQM)

R. Ashley Rawlins TD. DL.

authorHOUSE®

AuthorHouse™ UK Ltd.
500 Avebury Boulevard
Central Milton Keynes, MK9 2BE
www.authorhouse.co.uk
Phone: 08001974150

First published by AuthorHouse 7/24/2008

ISBN: 978-1-4343-7298-7 (sc)

Printed in the United States of America
Bloomington, Indiana

This book is printed on acid-free paper.

This book is dedicated to my wonderful parents; Mr William Joseph Emanuel Rawlins – Husband, Father, Builder -, Mrs Veronica Conciela Rawlins – Wife, Mother, Home-maker, Dressmaker -. Their teaching, support, guidance and encouragement are the major factors that influenced my life.

TABLE OF CONTENTS

PART TWO

PART THREE

PART FOUR

ACKNOWLEDGEMENTS

I would like to thank those friends and colleagues in the many organisations where I was involved, and who assisted me in preparing some of the information for this book, for their generosity in responding to my questionnaires and allowing me to draw on their experiences during the many discussions and interviews. Acknowledgements especially to; British Telecom Leeds Area, Leeds City Council, Nottingham City Council, Barnsley City Council, EnviroEnergy limited, British Airways, I.E.I. Leeds Limited (Part of the Conder Group) and the Rover Group – Birmingham – where I spent a full day with Directors and senior managers. A special thank you to the Directors and senior managers of some of the above organisations, who allowed me to meet and have discussions with junior staff during the normal working day and also for making sensitive business information available to me that is not normally available to the public. Acknowledgements also to the many authors of "TQM" whose works I have referenced in this book.

INTRODUCTION

In the 1980s, it became apparent that the Architects' Department of Leeds City Council was facing a crisis caused by the financial restrictions placed on Local Authority's spending by Central Government and the introduction of Compulsory Competitive Tendering (CCT) by Central Government into Local Authority Organisations.

By 1989 the Architects' Department had embarked on a rationalisation programme (despite trade union opposition) aimed at reducing its departmental costs to match the estimated long term budget forecast, which was expected to decrease, and to meet the demands of CCT. This programme entailed more than half of the workforce (middle managers and below) losing their jobs, through redeployments and early retirements. Senior Management was faced with the problem of developing an overall strategy that would allow the department to adapt to the changes in its external and internal environment.

Adapting was not just a question of coming to terms with a smaller organisation, but a more fundamental requirement to change existing attitudes and patterns of behaviour. During the early part of the prosperous 1960s an "us and them" attitude had emerged that had, by the mid 1970s, became positively entrenched, so much so that management and the other members of the workforce were constantly in conflict with each other, each side pursuing different objectives derived from self interest.

Decision-making had become highly centralised. This encouraged line-management to push problems for resolution, upwards to senior management, causing delays and misunderstanding, which lead to frustration at lower levels. First line-managers, under considerable pressure to achieve set targets, had become task orientated and at times unsympathetic towards the problems and frustrations of the other employees. This mode of action actually proved to be counter-productive because the harder managers tried to push work through, the more resistance they encountered from the workforce. Management, in exercising its right to manage, had excluded the majority of employees from meaningfully contributing to organisational objectives. These circumstances had combined to create a situation of "low trust" between management and other employees.

Senior Management realised that, if the organisation was to survive, management and other employees had to pull together in the direction of common organisational objectives. To change the situation, a strategy was developed that would, in essence, redefine the relationship between management and other employees; shifting it from a position of "low trust" to a position of "high trust".

The central theme of this strategy was employee involvement, and a major component of the overall change effort - besides a name change to The Leeds Design Consultancy - would be the introduction of a Total Quality Management (TQM) programme. TQM was seen as a vehicle for changing attitudes and behaviour at all levels by systematically involving managers and other employees in such multidiscipline groups specifically set up to analyse and solve project related problems.

This book set out to examine how successful the introduction of TQM into Local Authority and other large organisations, such as British Telecom, British Airways and Rover Group have been. The book is in four parts.

Part One draws on the research and experiences of others who are involved with TQM and, together with the literature available, seeks to give the reader an insight into the TQM concept before discussing issues of culture, implementation, and measures of TQM successes and failures.

Part Two uses the information collected in my research, to explain the background to the crisis that lead to the TQM programme being introduced as part of a major change strategy. This is essential to give the reader a clear understanding of both the circumstances that prevailed in some organisations before the TQM programme was introduced and the measures that were put in place, to complement the TQM programme. Part Two also compares the implementation stages of the TQM programme with the theoretical "deal", drawing the readers' attention to the shortcoming that research suggests will have a long term impact on the success of such quality systems and programmes. In Part Two, I also discuss the new structure for one local authority organisation, how the organisational structure has changed over the years and the reasons for those changes. Finally, the success of the TQM programme so far, is measured using the criteria established in Part One and responds to the question: How successful has the programme been in meeting its objectives?

In Part Three I discuss some research methods and their areas of application. I then used the in-depth interview research method for the studies related to this book and give reasons why I felt that it was the method most suitable for this work.

To interview all employees who were involved with the TQM programme would have been ideal but that was not practical. I felt that it was neither practical nor indeed necessary to interview all members of staff who were employed by the organisations of my interest at that time. I selected a number of people for the interviews so that I would achieve a variety of; backgrounds, levels of seniority, lengths of service and involvement in the organisations TQM programmes.

I used the information collected at the interviews to build the organisation's background contained in Part Three. This I felt was necessary to give the reader a good picture of the type of organisation, the management style, the organisational culture and an insight into how the culture of organisations have changed over the years.

Bias is a difficult problem to overcome but this was minimised by selecting interviewees whom I felt had integrity and would make honest and constructive comments. This had the added advantage of allowing me to compare my impressions of the interviewees before and after the introduction of the TQM programme. Therefore, Part Three concentrates on present and past members of the TQM programme. Through a series of interviews with selected people, I was able to establish their understanding of; the TQM concept, their expectations of the TQM programme after its implementation, whether they consider the TQM programme to be successful, their judgment of that success and their mental picture of the organisation as it went through the various changes.

Part Four draws the whole work together by examining the strengths and weaknesses of the TQM programme at both the implementation stage and operational level. From these observations I draw some general conclusions as to the effects of these elements on the programme's success. These findings are then compared with the results of my observations of other organisations that have pursued and introduced TQM programmes. In so doing, I was able to show the common indicators that could impact on any organisation where TQM programmes are being established. Observations of other organisations were obtained using; in-depth interviews in some cases – for organisations where I had some involvement in their TQM programmes -, in-depth interviews with managers and staff in organisations that I visited and published information in other cases. Finally, I go on to develop my own recipe for success of TQM programmes based on my general conclusions.

Part Four also investigate how schools can benefit from TQM. TQM is a system's approach for continuously improving the services and products that are offered to customers. In today's business and other organisation's environment, businesses and other organisations – including schools - that do not practice TQM can become; ineffective, inefficient and non-competitive very quickly. This march towards non-competitiveness can be avoided if; business leaders, teachers, school managers and school governors are helped to become

TQM practitioners. Therefore, the potential benefits for schools that embrace TQM can be far reaching.

Also included in Part Four is how TQM has developed in Chinese organisations and termed The Hong Kong (HK) TQM programme or the HK 5-S. The 5-S practice is useful because it helps everyone in the organisation to live a better life. It is the starting point of the HK TQM programme. In fact, many successful organisations, East and West, have already included some aspects of the 5-S in their routines without being aware of its existence as a formalised quality control technique. The Hong Kong Government is fully committed to promoting the 5-S practice in order to help its industries to improve their competitiveness. In the light of these HK TQM initiatives, I expect that the HK company that is reopening the Rover Group will introduce a similar TQM programme at Rover and that that initiative will create an organisational culture that will be different to what it was under the old Rover Group.

Evidence however, suggests that TQM can succeed where organisations have a well-established tradition of providing quality goods and services, for example; British Airways' Technical Workshops, Barnsley City Council and Nottingham City Council. Organisations – service or manufacturing – must strive to attain new quality bases, by raising the educational standards of the whole workforce. A tall order you may say, but it is not impossible. Statistical methodology, which is so very important in any organisation's TQM activities, may already exist in a quality conscious organisation. For such organisations, transferring those techniques and applying them to solve TQM problems would be much easier than for organisations with no tradition of quality.

While local authority organisations and some government departments my have difficulties in adapting TQM in areas such as social service and education and training, TQM programme can be beneficial to such organizations if properly planned and implemented. In those areas, TQM will have a better chance of success if TQM principles are viewed as an effective method of planning and implementing a change management programme. Top managers in such organisations could gain staff commitment for the TQM programme by ensuring that; TQM is a viable and effective change vehicle for the organisation, the organization is appropriate and its people are ready for TQM, the leadership is committed to the long-term plans of the organisation and the cultural change that is necessary.

PART ONE

THE TOTAL QUALITY MANAGEMENT CONCEPT

What is Quality?

Quality is often used to signify "excellence" of a product or service. We talk about "Rolls Royce quality" and "top quality". In some engineering organisations, the word "quality" may be used to indicate that a piece of metal conforms to certain physical dimension or characteristics often set down in the form of a particularly "tight" specification. If we are to define Quality in a way, which is useful in its management, then we must recognise the need to include in the assessment of quality, the true requirements of the customer.

Quality therefore, is simply meeting the customer requirements and others have expressed this in many ways, for example:

- "Fitness for purpose or use" (Juran) [1].

- "The totality of features and characteristics of a product or service that bears on its ability to satisfy stated or implied needs" (BS 4778, 1987) [2].

- "The total composite product and service characteristics of marketing, engineering, manufacturing, and maintenance through which the product and service in use will meet the expectation of the customer" (Feigenbaum) [3].

There is another word that we should define properly, "Reliability". Why does one shop at Marks & Spencer? "Quality and Reliability" comes back the answer. The two are used synonymously, often in a confused way. Clearly, part of the acceptability of a product or service will depend on its ability to function satisfactorily over a period of time, and it is this aspect of performance, which is given the name "reliability". It is the ability of the product or service to continue to meet the customer requirements. Reliability ranks with quality in importance, since it is a key factor in many purchasing decisions where alternatives are being considered. Many of the general management issues related to achieving product or service quality are also applicable to reliability. For example:

- Consistency of product

- Correct invoices

- On time delivery

- Frequency of delivery

- Speed of service

Introduction

Part One of this book introduces the Total Quality Management (TQM) concept by establishing a definition and then discussing the implications of the concepts origins. This leads to list of ingredients that are considered essential when implementing a Total Quality Management programme. Total quality authors suggest that these steps to implementation can determine the long-term success of the total quality programme. Measures of success, and the reasons why total quality programmes fail, are then highlighted before the implications of Part One for the rest of the book are stated.

Total Quality Management (TQM) – A Definition

What is TQM? It is necessary when writing a book of this nature to define for the reader key concepts, to establish from the outset a common understanding from which to proceed. In this respect I am no different from other authors.

Nigel Slack [4] argues that a good definition of TQM can be arrived at by examining the components of the name itself:

1. TOTAL means that everyone in the organisation is involved in the final product or service for the customer.

2. Quality must be defined in such a way that no one in the organisation can have any doubt what is meant by the word. Quality must never be subjective, and it must be clearly measurable. So, while one of the most common and useful definitions of quality is "meeting the customer's requirements" [5], these requirements must be stated, understood and quantifiable.

3. MANAGEMENT carries two implications. First, that "the TQM process has to start from the top" [6]. There has to be overall vision of the aims, principles and values of the organisation. Only top management is in a position to communicate it to everyone else. Second, management refers to a continuing process. Implementing TQM is not a one-off decision, it is a commitment to a long term attitude to work and that to be successful it needs continuous input, monitoring and support from the moment it is adopted and on into the future.

"The key objective of TQM is to change the overall culture of the organisation" [7]; to eliminate the view that errors are inevitable and that inspection and fire fighting are therefore part of everyday life, to create the feeling that everyone in the organisation is committed to total and continuous improvement.

Quality Management – An Organisational View Point

Within an organisation, management, employees, materials, facilities, processes and equipment all affect quality. The manager must be able to identify these aspects and seek to understand how they interact in the organisation. Once a strategy is developed, communicated, and the key variables affecting quality understood, the conversion function can take place. Services are generated and customers are satisfied. Some popular concepts of quality are:

- Quality is fitness for use.

- Quality is doing it right the first time and every time.

- Quality is the customer's perception.

- Quality provides a product or service at a price the customer can afford.

The key then, is the awareness of the need to improve and then to select improvement techniques with the best chance of success. An operating philosophy is required to establish and maintain an environment, which will result in never-ending improvement in the quality and the productivity of products and services throughout the organisation, its supply base and its dealer organisations. This requires the organisation to improve quality and productivity of every element of the business from planning to field service. It includes; all products and services, people relationships, attention to customers' needs, shareholders' investments, and management approaches. Finally, it must be "customer driven" [8].

Quality Management – Ideas and Approaches

Dr. Joseph Juran and Dr. W. Edwards Deming, specialists in Japanese Quality, suggest that as much as 85% of quality problems are management problems. (Deming: On Some Statistical Aids towards Economic Production [9]. Duran: Upper management and Quality [10]). Their views are that management, rather than employees, has the authority and tools to correct most quality ills. Philip B. Crosby's message is; "do it right first time" and "zero defects" [11]. Crosby argues that organisations spend about 20% to 35% of revenues doing things wrong and doing them over again. He argues that zero defects does not mean that people never make mistakes, but rather, that the organisation does not start out expecting them to make mistakes. Juran sees the key elements in implementing company wide strategic planning as identifying processes capable of meeting quality goals under operating conditions and producing continuing results in improved market share, premium prices and a reduction in error rates in the office and factory [12].

Juran's Nine Steps to Quality Goals:

1. Identify the customers.

2. Determine the needs of the customers.

3. Translate those needs into the company language.

4. Develop a product that can respond to those needs.

5. Optimise the product features so as to meet the company needs as well as customers' needs.

6. Develop a process, which is able to produce the product.

7. Optimise the process.

8. Prove that the process can produce the product under operating conditions.

9. Transfer the process to options.

Crosby's Fourteen Steps for Quality Improvement

1. Establish management commitment.

2. Form the quality improvement team from the representatives from each department.

3. Establish quality management throughout the company.

4. Evaluate the cost of quality.

5. Establish quality awareness by employees.

6. Instigate corrective action.

7. Establish an ad hoc committee for the zero defects programme.

8. Supervisor/employee training.

9. Hold zero defects day to establish the new attitude.

10. Employee goal setting should take place, on a 30, 60, 90-day basis.

11. Error cause removal should be set up to follow the collection of problems.

12. Establish recognition of those who meet the goals or perform outstandingly, by non-financial award programme.

13. Quality councils composed of quality professionals and team chairperson should meet regularly.

14. Do it all over again.

Deming's Fourteen Steps for Products & Services Improvement

1. Create constancy of purpose to improve product and service.

2. Adopt new philosophy for new economic age by management learning responsibilities and taking leadership for change.

3. Cease dependency on mass inspection. Require, instead, statistical evidence that quality is built in to eliminate the need for inspection on a mass basis.

4. End the practice of awarding business on a basis of price tag. Instead, depend on meaningful measures of quality, along with price.

5. Find problems. It is management's job to work continually on improving the system.

6. Institute modern methods of training on the job.

7. Institute modern methods of supervision.

8. Drive out fear so that every one may work effectively for the company.

9. Break down barriers between departments.

10. Eliminate numerical goals, posters and slogans that seek new levels of productivity without providing methods.

11. Eliminate work standards that prescribe numerical quotas.

12. Remove barriers that rob employees of their pride of workmanship.

13. Institute a vigorous programme of education and retraining.

14. Create a structure that will push on the prior 13 points every day.

I would like to add the following ideas:

1. Set up network enabling groups to share best practice.

2. Set up innovation groups to share experiences, either through face-to-face meetings, telephone conferencing or e-conferencing – computer -.

3. Set up a programme of support and training to help maximise support from other departments and organisations. This should include help with marketing strategies, workshops and research into the perceptions held by other departments and organisations.

4. Develop a business assessment toolkit to help improve efficiency and deliver value for money.

5. Develop partnerships with organisations at national and international levels to maximise opportunities for the organisation.

6. Offer more training in priority areas.

7. Review the perceptions about your work held by your customers and compare this with other departments and organisations.

8. Maximise opportunities for the organisation to work effectively with other departments.

9. Install quality systems such as BS5750, ISO 9002 or ISO 9001:2000 standard.

Comparison of Approaches

Dr. Deming has worked closely with Japanese businesses. His approach to quality improvement, analysis and statistics are widely accepted by Japanese businesses. In fact, the highest quality award in Japanese industry, "The Deming Prize", carries his name. According to Deming, responsibility for quality improvement lies at the manager's doorstep. The system is usually the cause for inefficiency and low quality according to Deming, and it is the manager's responsibility to work on the system - as workers in the system -. Deming's 14 principles stress design of product, specification of service offered, measurement by simple statistical methods, and action on the causes identified by these methods. He argues that variation is a major manufacturing problem and proposes the use of control charts to assist in evaluating variations [14].

Dr, Juran uses statistical analysis freely. His primary objective is to get management to help the company's management team develop the habit of annual improvement. In Juran's approach, continuing improvement is supplemented with the "break through" sequence, which is essentially an organised approach to problem identification, analysis and change based on this analysis.

The key to Juran's message is that management can and must seek continual improvement. In doing so, Quality will improve, along with other performance dimensions. Because competition with other firms and nations is so great, annual improvement, hands-on management, and training to institutionalise improvement, must all fit together in order to meet the competition for quality products and services [15].

Philip Crosby's book "Quality Is Free", explains his overall approach. He argues that; quality is free, it is not a gift, but it is free. What costs money are the unquality things, all the actions that involve not doing the jobs right first time. Quality is not only free, it is a profit maker. Every penny you don't spend on doing things wrong, or over, instead, becomes half a penny right on the bottom line [16].

Philip Crosby has been involved with training. The focus of this training is on conformance to requirements, prevention, the proper attitude towards quality and measuring quality as a cost of quality. Crosby's approach is based on attitudes and awareness; he focuses on management's role in using this approach to improve quality. Whereas Deming and Juran use analysis as a basis for their philosophies, Crosby's approach is behavioural. However, Crosby's methods seem to be quite effective; individual quality assurance executives, as well as major corporations such as IBM, have had good success with Crosby's approach.

Few studies have specifically investigated the relationship between quantity and quality of output. A popular view supported by Deming and Juran is, that any decrease in quantity would be more than offset by the reduction of waste due to the correct performance the first time. However, there seems to be no simple inherent relationship between these two factors, especially for such routine, repetitive tasks as typing or collating. Deming and Juran argued against Crosby's "zero defects" approach and suggest that posting defect statistics is misguided, and that instead, the defective elements in operations that generate a lot of defects should be tracked down. Juran claims that Crosby's "zero defect" approach does not help, since it is based on the idea that the bulk of quality problems arise because workers are careless and not properly motivated. Juran's and Deming's ideas conflict in terms of; identifying customers and their needs, establishing optimal quality goals, creating measurements of quality and producing continuing results in improved market share.

The Mission Statement

Making the Mission Statement is the task of top management [17]. Deming argues that, once the mission statement is formulated, it is the management's task to make sure that it becomes a living document. Everyone in the organisation must understand it and must integrate it into their day-to-day behaviour. If a lack of consistency can be communicated to the authority figure, and the authority receives it positively, then real communication can exist.

According to Deming, for positive communication to take place, the following four elements must exist:

1. The manager must communicate the desire to know when his/her behaviour is at odds with the mission statement.

2. The manager has to act on information received.

3. The manager should reward and encourage feedback behaviour.

4. Employees have to be willing to take the risk of giving management feedback.

An effective way of communicating to middle-level, lower-level managers and employees that top management intends that the mission statement be a living document, is to have every one write an interpretation of the statement.

New employees in the organisation should be aware of the importance of the organisation's mission statement.

Stakeholders should be aware of the organisation's mission so they can understand what the organisation is doing now and what it is planning for the future. The directors must be conversant with the organisation's Mission Statement.

Stakeholders for private sector organisations are usually the shareholders. For public sector organisations it is not as clear-cut because employees, the people requesting the goods or services and the people receiving the goods or services are all stakeholders.

Cultural Implications

Peter Drucker [18] wrote:

> "Management is not a mere discipline, but
> a culture with its own values, beliefs, tools
> and languages".

Pascale and Athos [19] develop this idea further by postulating that managerial sub-cultures lie within a nation's larger social culture and are therefore limited by it. Their argument is based on the distinctly different evolution of managerial cultures, in the East and West, from the core beliefs of society at large. On the one hand, Western society has developed separate institutions for government, church and military. From these institutions have evolved concepts of leadership and chain of command, which in turn have contributed to the imposition of beliefs and norms of behaviour. These ideas of what constituted social order were further developed during the industrial revolution with a greater emphasis on mass production and the development of the concept of the individual as a unit of production. Spiritual and social lives were divorced from the organisation. Western organisations concentrated on how to organise, delegate, reward, motivate and control resources and results. The culmination of these efforts was a style of management that over-emphasised the needs of the organisation at the expense of the needs of the individual. This philosophy has permeated managerial thinking and still persists today.

On the other hand, Eastern societies were more populous and so spiritual, public and private maters were, through necessity, more integrated. This social phenomenon was reflected on organisational tendencies to regard the task of control in the context of the whole of human needs, rather than the more narrowly defined relationships between labour and capital evident in the West.

This point is echoed by Bradley and Hill [20] who expressed the view that Japan's success may be due in part to features internal to Japanese firms, to their distinctive methods of organisation and management style. To support this view, they cite a number of characteristics that operate in Japanese organisations that, by Western standards, are quite different and reflect the beliefs of Japanese society at large. For example:

> There is a high degree of consensus supported by the policies that encourage group working and collective responsibility deliberately playing down the Western emphasis on individual effort and reward.

These views, whilst not conclusive, do suggest that organisations need a clear understanding of the cultural implications associated with TQM. By culture I mean both historical oriental development of TQM and the implications of existing organisational cultures, i.e. management style to impact on the success or failure of a TQM programme. Robert Heller [21] says; "BA's brand of TQM has not only cut costs but changed its culture". This suggests that there is a need for an in depth feasibility study, before deciding if the concept is right or wrong for any particular organisation.

Changes in Management Training

Management training in the UK is changing at a rapid rate. From the 1960s to the 1980s when UK industries, Universities and other management training establishments were keen to import their management training and management styles - especially in the manufacturing sector - from Japan and America, to the period after the 1990s to the twenty-first century when UK establishments are exporting management; systems, styles, concepts and thinking.

For many years UK establishments such as; Nottingham Business School, Sheffield Business School, Bradford University, Leeds Business School and others have been offering their management expertise to large manufacturing and service support organisations in the UK and abroad. They have been offering their services, not only to organisations and training establishments in developed countries, but also to those in developing countries too.

China is a good example of how UK management training establishments are helping to train and develop top managers for other countries. Although UK manufacturing organisations are losing out to China and other countries because of their low cost of labour, the UK still rank among the world's best in terms of training of the business leaders of tomorrow. China's manufacturing and support services are growing at an alarming rate. It is also importing a lot of its technologies from other countries and a lot of effort is being expended in training engineers and scientists, however, China is not growing senior managers at the rate required to match the rapid rate of increase that is taking place in the manufacturing and support services and China is looking to the UK to help it to train its top managers.

To address this problem - the short fall in management training for its industrial leaders - more than 600 Chinese manufacturing organisations have turned to Warwick University in the UK to train in excess of 200 graduates each year over a period of five years. One of China's biggest challenges is; being able to train its top managers quick enough to satisfy the pace of growth of its industrial and service support sectors. This is proving difficult if not impossible, and for this reason, a large number of Chinese companies have taken the decision that they would look to the UK to provide management training for their graduate engineers and scientists.

Providing post-graduate training for top managers from other countries may, in time, help to reduce criticisms that the UK is falling behind other developed countries in the skills race. Because of the shortage of skills in the UK, some large manufacturing companies are recruiting some of their staff with the necessary skills - key Staff - from other countries - Rolls-Royce for example - and others are moving some of their manufacturing overseas. However, even in these cases, those manufacturing companies are keeping their research and development centres in the UK.

How TQM Helps Organisations

Total Quality Management (TQM) is a way of managing to improve the effectiveness, flexibility, and competitiveness of an organisation as a whole. It applies just as much to service industries as it does to manufacturing. It involves whole organisations getting organised, in every department, every activity, and every single person, at every level. For an organisation to be truly effective, every single part of it must work properly together, because every person and every activity affects and are in turn affected by others. It is in this way that Japanese companies have become so competitive and so successful.

Organisations worldwide are regularly publishing statements that they are quality organisations. In the UK, many organisations of products and services are pursuing quality certification such as BS5750 and ISO9000. Quality statements can be seen displayed on notice boards and walls. Professional and non-professional publications regularly carry advertisements of Quality Consultants.

The UK "Industrial Revolution" took place more than a century ago. Perhaps the "Computer Revolution" happened in the early 1980s. But we are now in midst of the "Quality Revolution", a period of change affecting every type of; business, enterprise, organisation, and person. For any organisation, continuous quality improvement and cost reduction are essential if it is to stay in business as we strive to be part of a unified Europe.

Organisations compete on three issues: quality, price and delivery, according to Peters [22]. There cannot be many managers in the UK who remain to be convinced that quality is the most important of these. As quality improves, costs fall through reduction in failure and detection costs. The absence of quality problems also removes the need for the "hidden operations" devoted to dealing with failure and waste, and delivery performance benefits from increased output and higher productivity.

TQM reduces waste by removing the need for inspection. Detection of faults is replaced with faults prevention. The strategy of replacing detection with prevention can be adopted by organisations providing products or services.

TQM is also a method of reducing waste by involving every one in improving the way things are done. The techniques of TQM can be applied throughout an organisation so that people from different departments, with different priorities and abilities communicate with and help each other. These methods are equally useful in; finance, sales, marketing, design, accounts, distribution and production.

TQM helps organisations to:

1. Focus clearly on the needs of their markets.

2. Achieve top quality performance in all areas, not just in the product or service quality.

3. Operate the simple procedures necessary for the achievement of a quality performance.

4. Critically and continually examine all processes to remove non-productive activities and waste.

5. See the improvements required and develop measures of performance.

6.   Understand fully and in detail its competition and develop an effective competitive strategy.

7.   Develop the team approach to problem solving.

8.   Develop good procedures for communication and acknowledgment of good work.

9.   Review continually the processes to develop the strategy of never-ending improvement.

Causes of Quality Problems

Customers' -client departments and the public - expectations for a particular service, shape assessment of the quality of that service. When there is a discrepancy between customers' expectations and the management's understanding of customer expectations, perceived service quality will suffer. Management's failure to identify customer desires accurately will result in failure to meet quality standards or quality gap.

Even when management fully understands customer expectations, service-quality problems may occur. This is because management may believe that they know better about community requirements and that it is impossible or impractical to meet all of the expectations. I asked one Architect to explain his reason for specifying a building refurbishment that was different to the users' request. He said:

> "I wanted to have a contemporary design and the customer had problems understanding the ideas that I put forward, so I did it my way."

The organisation did not set its service specifications according to customer needs; instead, it allowed the service to suffer because of an assumption about who knows best.

In some cases, however, management does understand customer expectation and does set appropriate specifications - either informally or formally -, and still the service delivered by the organisation falls short. The difference between service specifications and the actual service is the service-performance gap. Unfortunately, this gap is common in professional organisations that provide technical and engineering services.

There are many opportunities for things to go wrong when the service organisation - the service provider - and the customer - client groups or public - interact, when both parties experience and respond to each other's; mannerisms, attitude, competence, mood, dress, language, etc. Similarly, there is more variability among service outcomes in professional/technical organisation service like an architect's department than, say, service outcomes from organisations like banks, because the powers vested in highly technical and professional people complicates quality control.

Service quality suffers when employees are unwilling or unable to perform the service at the level required. Willingness to perform may be described in terms of discretionary effort, the difference between the maximum amount of effort and care that an individual could bring to his/her job, and the minimum amount of effort required to avoid facing discipline. Employees may give 100% discretionary effort at the start of a new job but may be giving far less after only a few weeks or months. This can happen because they have had to deal with; a number of unreasonable customers, too many rules and regulations, and when they observe that not many of their colleagues are giving the job 100% effort. For example, during my appointment with Leeds City Council I was ridiculed by other managers and senior professionals for being too enthusiastic at work; "that is not the way we work here" one manager said to me.

In other cases, service organisations may not have the ability to perform at specified levels. The organisation may offer rates of pay that is insufficient to attract workers with the necessary skills or it may fail to train personnel adequately, or both. In addition, as a result of high turnover, or organisational changes – restructuring -, workers may be moved into higher-level positions before they are ready. For example, in a recent discussion with the Head of LDC, he said:

> "You will remember X, he was one of your Technicians when you were with us. Well he is still here, he has not gained any additional qualifications but I have bent the rules and given him a junior management position because of his loyalty."

These factors are typical of many service organisations and they can lead to poor service quality.

Maintaining service quality, then, depends not only on recognising customer desires and establishing appropriate standards but also on maintaining a work force of people who are willing and able to perform at specified levels.

Managers must determine what customers expect and how they expect to receive that quality of service. The consequent managerial tasks of planning, implementation and control should concentrate on both technical systems performance and functional operations performance. This should help prevent or minimise service quality failures.

Meeting the Requirements

If quality is meeting the customer requirements, then this has wide implications. The requirements may include; availability, delivery, reliability, maintainability and cost effectiveness, amongst many other features. The first item on the list of things to do is to find out what the requirements are.

Within organisations, between internal customers and suppliers, the transfer of information regarding requirements is frequently poor to totally absent. To achieve quality throughout an organisation, each person in the organisation must interrogate every interface as follows:

Customers

- Who are the immediate customers?

- What are their true requirements?

- How to find out what the requirements are?

- How can the organisation measure its ability to meet the requirements?

- Does the organisation have the necessary capability to meet the requirements?

- Does the organisation continually meet the requirements?

- How does the organisation monitor changes in the requirements?

Suppliers

- Who are the organisation's immediate suppliers?

- What are the organisation's true requirements?

- How does the organisation communicate its requirements?

- Do the organisation's suppliers have the capability to measure and meet the requirements?

- How does the organisation inform its suppliers of changes in requirements?

Commitment to Quality

To be successful in promoting organisation efficiency and effectiveness, TQM must be company-wide and it must start at the top with the Chief Executive, or equivalent, the most senior directors and management, who must all, demonstrate that they are serious about quality. Middle management has an important role to play. They must not only grasp the principles of TQM, they must go on to explain it to people for whom they are responsible, and ensure that their own commitment is communicated. Only then will TQM spread effectively throughout the organisation. This level of management must also ensure that the efforts and achievements of their subordinates obtain the; recognition, attention and reward that they deserve. It cannot be said too often that to be successful, TQM must involve everyone in all departments.

Within each and every department of the organisation at all levels, starting at the top, basic changes of attitude will be required to operate TQM. If top management of the organisation do not recognise and accept their responsibilities for the initiation and operation of TQM, then these necessary changes will not happen. Systems and techniques are important in TQM, but they are not the primary requirements. It is more an attitude of mind, based on pride in the job, and requiring total commitment from the management, which must then be extended to all employees at all levels in all departments.

Management's commitment must be an obsession, not lip service. It is possible to detect real commitment; it shows at the point of operation.

TQM is user driven; it cannot be imposed from outside the organisation, as perhaps a quality system stand or statistical process control. This means that the ideas for improvement must come from those with the knowledge and experience of the methods and techniques, and this has massive implications for training and follow-up. TQM is not a cost-cutting or productivity improvement device and must not be used as such. Although the effects of a successful TQM programme will include these benefits, TQM is concerned chiefly with changing attitudes and skills so that the culture and the norm are operating "right first time".

Three Major Components

The organisation, which believes that the traditional quality control techniques, and the way they have always been used, will result in total quality, is wrong. Employing more inspectors, tightening up standards, developing correction, repair and rework teams does not promote quality. Traditionally, quality has been regarded as the responsibility of the "Quality Control" department, and still it has not been recognised in some organisations that many quality problems originate in the service or administration areas. This occurs because their management systems are viewed in terms of internal dynamics between; marketing, design, production, distribution, accounting, etc. A change is required to a larger system, which also encompasses and integrates the business interests of the customers and suppliers.

In addition to the management commitment requirement, which has already been discussed, there are three major components of TQM:

1.   A documented quality management system.

2.   Statistical Process Control (SPC).

3.   Teamwork.

A documented system

"Consistency can only be achieved if we ensure that, for every product or each time a service is performed; the same materials, the same equipment, the same method or procedures, are used in exactly the same way, every time" [23]. The process will then be under control. This is the aim of a good quality management system, to provide the operator with consistency and satisfaction in terms of; methods, materials and equipment.

Statistical Process Control (SPC)

SPC is not a tool kit. It is a strategy for reducing variability, the cause of quality problems; variation in product or service, time of delivery, in ways of doing things, in materials, in everything. Control by itself is not sufficient. TQM requires that the process should be improved continually by reducing its variability. "Total Quality is all about Continuous Improvement" [24]. Studying all aspects of the process using the following questions brings this about:

- "Could we do this job more consistently and on target"? [25] [26]

- Are we capable of doing the job correctly?

- Do we continue to do the job correctly?

- Have we done the job correctly?

Teamwork

The complexity of most of the processes, which are operated in; industry, commerce and services, place them beyond the control of any one individual. The only way to tackle problems concerning such processes is through the use of some form of teamwork. The use of the team approach to problem solving has many advantages over allowing individuals to work separately on problems. The following are some advantages:

- A greater variety of problems may be tackled, which is beyond the capacity of any one individual, or even one department.

- The problems are exposed to a greater diversity of; knowledge, skills and experience.

- The approach is more satisfying to team members and boosts morale.

- The problems, which cross-departmental or func-tional boundaries, can be dealt with more easily.

- The recommendations are more likely to be implemented than individual suggestions.

- Most of these rely on the premise that people are most willing to support any effort in which they have taken part and help to develop.

Teamwork devoted to quality improvement, changes independence to interdependence through; improved communications, trust and a free exchange of; ideas, knowledge, data and information. However, employees will not be motivated towards continual improvement in the absence of the following:

- Commitment to quality from the management.

- An organisational quality climate.

- A team approach to quality problems.

Planning the Implementation of TQM

The task of implementing TQM can be daunting and the management team faced with this may draw little comfort from the "quality gurus", because different organisations require different approach when implementing a TQM programme. The first decision is where to start and this can be so difficult that many organisations never get started.

The preliminary stages of understanding and commitment are vital first steps, which also form the foundation of the whole TQM structure. Some organisations skip these phases, believing that they have the right attitude and awareness, when in fact there are some fundamental gaps in their quality creditability. These will soon lead to insurmountable difficulties.

While an intellectual understanding of quality provides a basis for TQM, it is clearly only the planting of the seed. The understanding must be translated into commitment, policies, plans and action for TQM to germinate. Making this happen requires not only commitment, but also a competence in the mechanics of quality management, and in making changes. Without a strategy to implement TQM through systems, capability and control, the expended effort will lead to frustration.

The implementation begins with the drawing up of a quality policy statement, and the establishment of the appropriate organisational structure, both for managing and encouraging quality through teamwork. Collecting information on how the organisation operates, including the cost of quality, helps to identify the prime areas in which improvement will have the largest impact on performance. Planning improvement involves all managers but a critical early stage involves putting quality management systems in place to drive the improvement process and make sure that problems remain solved, using structured corrective action procedure.

Once the plans and systems have been put into place, the need for continued education, training and communication becomes paramount. Organisations, which try to change the; quality culture, management systems, procedures, or control methods without effective two-way communication, will experience the frustration of being a "cloned" type of organisation, which can function but inspires no confidence in being able to survive the changing environment in which it lives.

If good understanding of quality and how it should be managed already exists, there is top management commitment, a written quality policy and a satisfactory organisational structure, then, the planning stage may begin straightaway. When implementation is completed, priorities amongst the various projects must be identified. For example, a quality system, which conforms to the requirements of ISO 9000 or BS 5750 series may already exist and systems for quality will not be a major task, but introducing a quality-related costing system may well be. A review of the current performance in all the areas, even those that are well established, should be part of normal operations to ensure continuous improvement.

Quality Gurus

Although the Quality Gurus' messages cover the series of steps to TQM implementation, there is some disagreement between the gurus, such as the particular warnings on slogans and on the naïve use of Quality Circles. However, there are considerable agreement between the gurus as to the problem, aims and approach but there is no comprehensive and coherent model. It seems to me that the work of intellectuals such as Professor D. S. Morris and R, H. Haigh of Sheffield Business School, Professor J. S. Oakland of the University of Bradford and others, is bringing the Quality Gurus' series of prescriptions together to provide us with comprehensive and coherent models. For example; the figure below is a model developed by Professor D. S. Morris and R. H. Haigh.

The model is based on Five Agreed Principles of TQM:

1. The customer is king. (A. V. Feigenbaum; "Total Quality Control" 1983).

2. Everyone participates in Total Quality Control (TQC). (K. Ishikawa; "what is total Quality Control"? 1985).

3. Quality measurement is essential. (Philip Crosby; "Quality is Free" 1979).

4. Align corporate systems to support TQC. (M. Imai; "Kaizen" 1986).

5. Constantly strive for improvement. (W. Edwards Deming; "Out of Crisis" 1986).

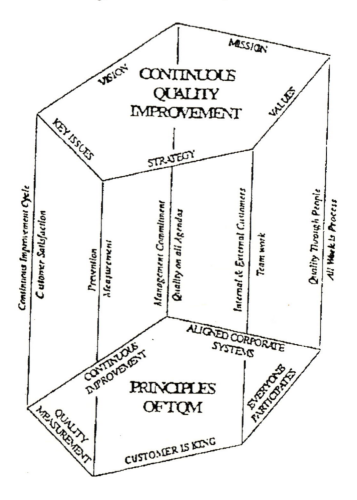

References

1. J. M. Juran: Quality Control Handbook, 3rd Edition, McGraw-Hill Book Company, New York 1979.

2. BS 4778, 1987 (ISO 8402, 1986) Quality Vocabulary, Part 1 International Terms.

3. F. Feigenbaum: Total Quality Control, 3rd Edition, McGraw-Hill Book Company, New York, 1983.

4. Nigel Slack: The Manufacturing Advantage Achieving Competitive Manufacturing Operations. Mercury Books 1991.

5. Terry Hill: Production / Operations Management. Prentice Hall 1983.

6. John E. F. Jarvis: Director Quality Strategy / UKC, British Telecom Tools and Techniques Handbook Section 1. Jan. 1988.

7. W. E. Deming: Quality, Productivity and Competitive Position. MIT Center for Advanced Engineering Study, Cambridge, Mass., 1982.

8. W. E. Deming: See reference 7.

9. H. S. Gitlow and S. J. Gitlow: The Deming Guide to Quality and Competitive Position. Prentice-Hall INC, Inglewood Cliffs, NJ, 1987.

10. J. M. Juran and F. M. Gryna: Quality Planning and Analysis, 2nd Edition, McGraw-Hill Book Company, New York, 1979.

11. P. B. Crosby: Quality is Free. McGraw-Hill Book Company, New York, 1979.

12. J. M. Juran: Upper Management and Quality, 4th Edition. Juran Institute INC. New York 1983.

13. W. E. Deming: Out of the Crisis, MIT Center for Advanced Engineering Study, Cambridge, Mass., 1986. Steve Flax: An Auto Man Turns Up. Wren-Lambert, Fortune 3, Number 5. Gitlow and Gitlow: See reference 9.

14. H. S. Gitlow and S. J. Gitlow: See reference 9.

15. J. M. Juran: See references 10 and 12.

16. P. B. Crosby: See reference 11.

17. W. E. Deming: See reference 7.

18. P. F. Drucker: Management. Harper and Row, New York, 1972.

19. P. T. Pascale and A. G. Athos: The Art of Japanese Management. Sedgwick and Jackson, 1986.

20. K. Bradley and S. Hill: After Japan. The Quality Circle Transplant and productive Efficiency, British Journal of Industrial Relations.

21. Robert Heller: How BA Engineered its Turnaround. BIM, Management Today, September 1992.

22. T. J. Peters and R. H. Jr. Waterman: In Search of Excellence. Harper and Row publishers, New York 1982.

23. The International Standards Organisation (ISO) Standards 9000 Series (Equivalent to BS 5750 1987).

24. John E. F. Jarvis: Director Quality Strategy / UKC. British Telecom Tools and Techniques Handbook, Section 1, 1982.

25. J. S. Oakland: Statistical Process Control. Heinemann, Oxford, 1989.

26. F. Price: Right First Time. Gower, London, 1985.

PART TWO

ORGANISATIONAL BACKGROUND – LEEDS CITY COUNCIL "ARCHITECTS"

Introduction

This section examines the events leading up to the decision to introduce a "Total Quality Management" (TQM) programme in the Architects' Division of Leeds City Council in April 1991.

Most of the details in this section are based on information obtained during various interviews, which I had with a number of employees who were employed by Leeds City Council before and after the implementation of the TQM programme.

These events are set against a backcloth of how the division operated during the 1970s and 1980s. This insight is essential to enable the reader to appreciate the conditions - particularly management style and the various reorganisations plus relocations - that prevailed, prior to the implementation of the TQM programme. It is my firm belief that these conditions considerably influence the success or failure of the TQM programme.

Historical Background

Early Changes

In 1975 the organisation was designated "Architecture and Landscape Department" with staff in excess of 400 personnel. This included, separately managed Electrical Engineering and Mechanical Engineering sections. Separately managed electrical and mechanical sections have for a very long period of time been a major topic of discussion in the Engineering Industry.

The argument was that Electrical and Mechanical Engineering sections should amalgamate and be managed by the Head of Building Engineering Services. Although many industries - including some City Councils - adopted this procedure, it took nearly two decades before Leeds City Council adopted this procedure. This meant that Engineering within Leeds City Council was not in synchronism with; other engineering organisations, industries, or organisations with which it was in daily operational contact.

The first major change occurred in 1980/81, caused by a change in the political majority and leadership from Conservative to Labour on the Leeds City Council. There had been suggestions and discussions by the politicians on the City Council, over a long period of time, about amalgamating the Architect's Department and the Department of Public Works. However, the professional group - Architects and Engineers - objected very strongly to this suggestion, arguing that a professional group should not be employed in the same organisation as a contractor group - Public Works - because there would be conflict of interests. Due to these difficulties, that amalgamation never took place.

In addition to the above argument, Central Government were determined to make Public Works Departments be more accountable, because for many years private contractors have been complaining about the unfairness in the City Councils' procedures of awarding contracts, when they have contracting groups within City Councils, operating in the same arena as the professional groups that are awarding the contracts. So there have always been a lot of pressure on City Councils to; either not have Public Works Departments or to make them accountable in the same way as a private contractor.

Central Government decided that Public Works Departments should be made accountable in the same way as private contractors. This meant that in future, Public Works Departments were required to compete with Private Contractors for City Councils' contracts. A number of City Councils - including Leeds City Council - did every thing in their power to try and soften the impact of this decision. In Leeds City Council, a number of simultaneous activities occurred; there was the above decision by Central Government, there was a change of political majority and leadership on the City Council - Conservative to Labour -, and there had been a stated objective to move City Council's Departments out of expensive city centre offices.

The Department of Architecture and Landscape was moved from expensive office space in Dudley House, located in the centre of Leeds, to less expensive accommodation in Sweet Street, Leeds and was amalgamated with the Public Works Department.

One of the advantages of moving to Sweet Street was, if there was a fee earning professional operational organisation, such as the Department of Architecture and Landscape, which could be said to be operating as part of the Public Works Department, Then the impact of accountability on the Public Works Department is diffused because the organisation could look at its operating overheads and decide how those overheads will be allocated throughout the organisation.

There was a requirement, that the size of the department should be reduced, because the City Council's capital programme was getting smaller. This was achieved with the aid of a major early retirement programme, which saw the department's size reduced by about 250 employees by the middle of 1981. The smaller department was then relocated to accommodation in Sweet Street.

A new building was constructed at considerable expense to accommodate the Department of Architecture and Landscape. It became part of Public Works department but retain its separate identity in the sense that it operated as a Division within Public Works Department.

The Director of Public Works was the supreme, and in the same way that an organisation would have a construction division with an Assistant Director at its head, the Department of Architecture and Landscape became part of Public Works, with an Assistant Director at its head.

The discussions, debates and arguments about the unfairness of having the professional design group, who put work out to tender, operating within the same arena as the contracting group, who tenders for that work, continues. The Architects Department continued to operate in the same way as it did before the amalgamation, except that it had fewer employees. It was not even subject to the control of Public Works Department and its Committee.

Following the above changes, were a series of reorganisations, some were caused by the reduction in staffing levels together with a smaller capital programme. However, others were to do with restructuring, which had become the latest fad on the management scene. Within Leeds City Council, like most public and local authority organisations, one restructure followed so close on the heals of another, that the first one was never finished. To some extent it seems to me, that the philosophy was; if you commence a programme of restructuring, which possibly is not going to be wholly successful, the thing to do was to start another restructure before the failure of the first, becomes apparent.

Changing Climate

Local authority organisations started a series of restructuring exercises - not only the Architects' Departments, but elsewhere -, which was generally intended to meet the changing climate. The changing climate in this case, was caused by Central Government's determination, and they made their intention clear, that those areas of Local Government that could, would be made to compete with the private sector organisations for local authorities' works.

Whilst Architects' Departments were not, and to my knowledge are still not mandated by Central Government to be in the same position as a Direct Labour Organisation – DLO - or in the same way as; Public Works, Leisure, Parks and others, Leeds City Council, nevertheless, was disposed to move in this direction. This was so that, if Central Government imposed the requirement, they would already be part way there. When Central Government did the first tranch, they started with Public Works and imposed a requirement, that Public Works be made accountable. There were a number of different ways to deal with this, one of which was; the integration of other areas of activities into Public Works, with the effect that its accounts would be diffused and so reduce the impact on Public Works.

Central Government agreed to an arrangement where Local and Public Authority departments were expected to compete with Private Sector organisations for Central Government and City Council's work. They initially identified six areas of activities; public Works, Leisure Services, Parks Services, Building Cleaning, Refuse Collection and Street Cleaning.

They declared, at that time, that this list was not exhaustive and that there were other areas which they intend to apply the same requirements to. One such area was Architecture.

This was an obvious choice because it presented itself ready for the kind of competitive activity being encouraged by Central Government; however, it was not added to the list at this early stage. Architecture was added to the list of service areas about two years later, although no date was set for it to start operating competitively with the Private Sector.

Some Local Councils, including Leeds City Council, disposed themselves towards organising those departments that were in the category targeted by Central Government, so that they could be seen to be moving positively towards making those departments competitive, rather than waiting until Central Government add them to the list. That would cause major problems for local authorities if they were not already prepared for such actions.

All of this was happening in the background, which was one of the reasons given for much of the restructuring exercises that went on. The amalgamation or integration of Electrical and Mechanical Engineering into the Building Services Group whilst accommodated in new buildings at Sweet Street was one such restructuring exercise.

Political Requirements

The Architects' Department continued to operate much the same as it did before restructuring, as a Division of Public Works. There were changes to some functions; for instance, the Surveyors Group, which had previously been a Public Works activity, became part of the Architects' Department, but continued to operate as a separate function.

The political pot was boiling and it seems that staff and a number of senior and junior managers were unaware of the extent to which this pot was boiling. At this stage, came the requirement that the design and contract functions should be separated. This was a political decision, made by the ruling Labour Group, and it brought to a head the various arguments and discussions about having the professional specifying group working shoulder to shoulder with another group that was required to tender competitively for the work being put out to tender by the specifying group.

The political pot came to the boil quickly and suddenly. The Architects' Department were required to disassociate itself from Public Works and that led to the decision to transfer the Architects' Department to another building in a location away from Sweet Street where Public Works were located. The Architects' Department were moved to Merrion House located in the centre of Leeds City.

This decision was required because Central Government were becoming stricter with Local Authorities, especially with regards to how their Direct Labour Organisations – DLO - accounted for themselves. Central Government would no longer tolerate a DLO having within it, professional specifying groups who were putting work out to tender on a competitive basis. They did not want the two functions to be under the same management or even to be collocated in the same building, so the Architects' Department had to move to a new location.

Confrontation

The political decision to move the Architects' Department to Sweet Street was poor and ill thought out, however, Leeds City Council had this idea, that if they amalgamated the

Architects' Department and Public Works under a single management, then the decision by Central Government to make DLOs, such as Public Works, tender competitively for their work would have no significant impact on The Public Works Department. This assumption turned out to be wrong because Central Government were determined not to allow those two departments to operate under a single management structure. So, the Architects Department did not have a choice, they had to move.

The proposed move and changes were plagued by difficulties; with elected members on the Leeds City Council getting involved in day-to-day management activities in areas where they have neither qualifications, skills or experience, by endless delays caused by conflicts and lack of cooperation between staff and between different trade unions, poor leadership and bad planning.

The move of the Architects' Department to Merrion House caused a lot of trouble because; the intention was that the Architects' Department would move to Merrion House and take the premises occupied by Social Services Department, who resisted the move. The Architects' Department resisted this move also and as a consequence of these, sprung up a strong union group who carried the remainder of the department with them to resist the move. They laid down a number of conditions, which they wanted the Council to meet before the move took place. This was on the basis that the strongest hand is before the game is plaid rather than after.

The situation became one of confrontation between the two departments - represented by their respective trade unions - and the politicians on Leeds City Council, who were insisting on the move. Social Services Department did not resist the move as much as the Architects' Department, but they - Social Services Department - did not want to move from the centre of Leeds to the new location in Sweet Street. It seems that they did not like that at all.

The situation reached crisis, when the Leader of Leeds City Council gave a directive, requiring that the move took place within one week of the date of that directive. The move was to be carried out over the period of one weekend.

It is not surprising that this crisis came about, because the liberty of one group depends on the restraint of another group. In this case, the common foundation upon which rests; liberty, equality and morality was nonexistent. No one complains that captains give orders and soldiers obey them or that coach drivers work to a timetable laid down by their managers. For if captains and managers command, they do so by virtue of their office and it is by virtue of their office that their instructions are obeyed. They are not masters, as some managers' thinks they are, but fellow servants for those whose work they direct. In this case, they are public servants. Power is not conferred upon them by birth or wealth, but by the position, which they occupy in the productive system. However, if this power is use fairly and with sensitivity and respect, their subordinates may grumble at its use but will not dispute the need for its existence.

R. H. Tawney argues that "inequality of power is tolerated; when the power is used for a social purpose approved by the community, when its existence is not arbitrary, but grounded by settled rules and when the commission can be revoked, if its terms are exceeded".

Following this directive was a statement of non-corporation by the Architects' Department, made through their trade union. Some people were determined no to assist in the move, others saw that the move was going to take place any way, and felt that the sensible thing to do was to try to organise things, so that the move did not have too devastating an effect, but they were nevertheless, afraid of the consequences of their actions relative to the Union movement.

Those employees, who held management positions, had a conflict of responsibilities, because first of all; they were members of the Trade Union, and secondly, managements' function is to manage the smooth efficient operation of an area of the City Council's work for which they are employed. If they all stood aside and did nothing, then the result would be chaos. It seems that is largely what happened.

The Political Leaders/Strategic Managers, throughout this process seems to have forgotten the department's values as set out by themselves, as follows:

- Looking After Leeds – We are committed to improving the quality of life in Leeds and want to inspire pride in our city and communities. We will work with our partners, build on our success and protect our city for future generation.

- Putting Customers First – We will make sure our services meet the needs of our customers. We will communicate clearly and work hard to find out and respond to our customers needs. We are committed to providing excellent services that are value for money.

- Treating People Fairly – We valve the diversity of our communities to ensure that every one shares in the city's success. We will tackle discrimination and improve access to our services, especially to those with the greatest need.

- Valuing Colleagues – We know that the good work of our colleagues is key to providing excellent services. We will support colleagues and encourage them to work creatively.

The Management Group did what they could themselves but the City Council sent in from outside, a group of people to physically move the department's furniture, equipment and stationary from Sweet Street to Merrion House. This work was carried out over a weekend. Staff walked out of the workplace at Sweet Street on the Friday, having done nothing to assist. They packed nothing for the move, not even their drawings, books, catalogues etc. Those who were sensible took with them all their personal possessions, but they did nothing towards the smooth move of equipment and stationary. As a consequence of this said a member of the Senior Management Group:

"Things were in a horrendous mess. All the furniture and all the equipment for doing the job were thrown on the floor, much of it was broken as a result of rough handling by the people who were brought in from other departments".

Senior Managers did what they could to supervise the move. They felt that they were not able to stand back and do nothing because they realised, the less participation there was, the worse the situation would be and also the more difficult it would be to re-establish proper working conditions after the event. There was an estrangement between management and the rest of the staff because, the other staff regarded managers as members of the same union, having the requirement to adopt the same attitude and yet, managers, from their positions felt that they had no choice but to protect the department's interest.

It seems to me rather surprising that a group of employees, recruited because of their; intellect, skills and innovative thinking did not see the damage they were doing to their department and also to their careers by not taking care of their equipments and other materials. There were drawings and specifications that were incomplete and related to various projects for which they were responsible. How did they expect to pick up the lead on those projects the following Monday? These professional employees were; Architects, Electrical Engineers, Mechanical Engineers, Civil Engineers, Quantity Surveyors, their related Technicians and Assistants.

I joined that organisation as a Senior Design Manager in 1988 during its preparation for the introduction of a TQM programme. I spent a large proportion of my time during my first six months with the organisation, getting a number projects back on track. Other projects were in such mess, in terms of slippage and poor quality of work, on some sites, due to lack of control, that they over-ran by several months. I asked several clients for their views on the condition of their projects and without exception the statements were:

"I will never trust your engineers again. They think only of themselves and are not committed to their work. In the future I may consider going to private architects and engineers".

Uncertainty

The Architect's Department were not a primary essential function of the City Council so the City Council could have taken a fairly stern view that if that department's staffs were to turn up and say they could not work, the City Council would say, "well don't". At that time the staff of the Architect's Department did not really know what they were because, they had not been formally separated from Public Works Administration.

Before they became part of Public Works, they had their own committee. When they became part of Public Works they reported to the same committee as Public Works. When they left Public Works, they were nothing because, they had no committee, and they were not a substantial department and were still administered by Public Works. Yet, the requirement was that they should be separated entirely from Public Works.

They operated for a short period of time with that uncertainty, used the administration of Public Works but, became responsible - not officially - to the Director of administration. The City Architect reported to the Director of Administration but still relied upon Public Works to give his group administrative support and still answerable/reported to the same committee as Public Works did. This whole area of work was in a horrendous mess. This mess seems to have been caused by politicians trying to manage functions without the experience or skills to manage.

It would have been much better if the politicians stuck to the task of formulating policies, with the task of managing carried out by managers. Staff and clients might have been saved a lot of heartaches if the Senior Managers were of stronger character and stood up to the politicians. However, they were all nearing retirement and the thought of having to find alternative employment would have been daunting.

Gradually the links with Public Works were released. They became more responsible to the Director of Administration and began to function more as an independent department but they were not a fully-fledged department.

One Architect said:

> "We were in the wilderness in administrative terms".

In a sense, it was similar to having been transferred as a division from Public Works to Administration, but it was not as clear-cut as that. They did not have the same common ground for interaction with Administration as they had with Public Works. The only link was that the City Architect reported to the Director of Administration and that his contact with political committees was through Administration rather than Public Works.

There were lots of speculations about what was going to happen. Following the move, all employees had to cope with getting things working again, not an easy task considering the mess that staff had allowed essential items to get into. The Union by this time saw sufficient sense to withdraw their non-cooperation and members of staff reluctantly turned their hands towards getting things into working order. Union activities were still going strong at this stage and I understood that politicians saw this as being antagonistic towards the City Council's decision.

The Architect's Department had estranged itself from the sympathy of the politicians because it had taken a stand against them. It had been unsuccessful with that stand, yet it had made itself unpopular.

Around this same period when all of this was going on, it was decided that City Council departments should look more seriously towards establishing groups that could compete with outside interests such as private organisations doing similar work or providing similar services.

Clearly, circumstances in the organisation's external environment had changed dramatically over a short period of time. Prior to this, Leeds City Council operated in a relatively stable environment, consequently changes in strategy were operational in nature, with major shifts being unnecessary. Now there had been a "global" [1] change in the environment that required a conscious re-alignment of internal resources. New strategies had to be formulated over a relatively short period of time to shift the overall direction of the organisation. Clearly, senior managers had to move quickly in response to the situation and develop strategies that would create an environment that was conducive to change.

> "Constant change can affect the morale and motivation of all concerned. Managers are under pressure to deliver, to bring changes into effect whilst continuing to motivate not only themselves but also their teams. Employees will, understandably, feel threatened by change and may feel insecure as a result of proposals, which place jobs in jeopardy. Elected members find it difficult to maintain their traditional role and will often find it all but impossible to juggle with competing priorities in a climate of increasing financial restrictions" [2].

In my recent discussions with a number of senior managers, staff and politicians it is clear to me that the following lessons have not been learned:

- Managers and planners should not expect all colleagues to embrace changes, especially when they are directly affected by those changes.

- Staff reacts more favourable to change if they are experimenting and finding better ways of doing things rather than just planning and talking about them.

- Senior managers must get rid of obstacles to change and do so in the shortest time possible.

- The organisation must; think, behave and act as a team.

- Senior managers should stand by what they believe in.

- Timing and effective communication are of the utmost importance.

- Organisations must take time to celebrate excellence and achievement whenever the opportunity arises.

Influences on the Objectives

The cost of capital is not the only influence on the objectives. Some other influences are: -

The cost and location of property, for example, Technical Services is located in Merrion House and besides being cramped for space, it is very expensive and the department is hoping to move to other property in the near future.

The department hopes to achieve steady growth and improvement in the condition of life rather than having a super year followed by a bad year.

There are some constraints and bureaucracies in the organisation, which puts it at a disadvantage when competing with other organisations.

The values of society are a major influence; attitudes to work, authority, equality and a whole range of other important issues are constantly shaped and changed by society at large. Leeds City Council is labour controlled but the corporate strategies are similar to those put forward by the Conservative controlled Central Government so a culture change caused by a change of Government will not affect its corporate plans.

The organisation has shown large resource excess mainly in staffing level.

To overcome the problems outlined above the decision was taken to "restructure the Technical Services department by rationalisation". This decision was taken at the Strategic Planning level - Politicians and Senior Management Team - without consultation with staff or staff representatives - respective trade unions -. This is rather surprising, considering the very low morale displayed by staff and their lack of trust for managers at the strategic level because of the lack of consultation over a number of recent organisational changes.

A meeting was held to outline the plan to staff, who were employed in the Technical Services Department. This was not; a consultation, discussion of proposals, outlining aims, objectives or an effort to gain staff confidence. In a sense, it was completely opposite. The speakers were; the Chair of Technical Services Committee and the Director of Administration. Remember I said earlier that Technical Services and Administration had nothing in common.

The first speaker was the Director of Administration, who stated:

> "I am here to outline the proposal for restructuring, I will not speak with union representatives and I will not answer questions from the union".

He then explained the proposal to reduce staff level from 250 to 100. This he argued, will put the department on a better footing to compete with private organisations, and will be achieved by voluntary early retirement, voluntary redundancies and redeployment.

The second speaker, a Labour Councillor and Chair of the Technical Services Committee, suggested that people should start looking for other jobs. He stated:

> "No one has a right to a job and any one who thinks he has, is living in cloud cuckoo land".

He added:

> "The new structure will be posted on the notice board and if your name does not appear against any of the positions then, you are not included in the new structure".

Not a comment that would motivate even the most committed and loyal staff. A good lesson in bad management or maybe just being foolhardy. I was appointed about four months after this meeting was held to help clear up some of the mess caused by these poorly thought out decisions.

It seems to me that at this stage, no attempt had been made at proper communication or negotiation. There was no evidence of proper strategic planning or delegation of tasks in an effort to gain staff commitment to the implementation of the required organisational changes. It appears that some decisions were taken irrationally out of pride and embarrassment due to previous experience; such decisions could not be classed as good management. Decisions should not be taken out of pride, sentiment or embarrassment, but out of pure strategy. Strategy here suggests that there was a requirement to change to meet Central Government's Legislations in terms of competing with private organisations for City Council's Contracts. To achieve this and be successful required a more slim-line and efficient organisation; therefore, what were required of Strategic Managers were; calmness, patience, organisational skills and the ability to lead without stepping on toes.

Change should be introduced with the minimum of friction or conflict and the maximum of cooperation but the actions of the strategic Managers was provocative and an irresponsible use of power. In this organisation, the interests of the workers are identical to those of the public who are their clients. The general public as well as the organisation will suffer when that organisation is antiquated and inefficient. Therefore, they should be equally concerned if the necessary measures are not taken to modernise the organisation and make it more efficient. No individual on his/her own can hope to carry out such modernisation, the complex fabric of environmental, economic and social arrangements, on which the attainment of successful change depends. It all hinges on the cooperative actions of staff and managers alike, as they participate and work together to undertake that task.

This Machiavellian style of management, which attempts to influence situations, to create desired outcomes, or to change organisation's effectiveness by using; power, status, manipulation, guile etc has been successful in the past, but is now, well outdated and is no longer working in this type of organisation as well as it once did – say in the early 1950s to the late 1970s. The premise of this approach is that those involved in, or affected by the changes planned, must be as little involved in the strategy as possible. By so doing, by the time they realise what is happening it will be far too late to do anything about it and they will have no option but to accept the new situation. There are still some organisations where employees expect to be managed in this way and tolerate it because it gives them the comfort of knowing that someone else is taking the important decisions. However, in professional organisations, such as this one under discussion, employees enjoy taking decisions; they are highly motivated and innovative so such management style is unlikely to be successful.

I believe that the British Army is one of the best training grounds for managers and during my early stages as a Commissioned Officer I had instilled in me that my most important assets are the soldiers who are put under my command. Treat your soldiers with courtesy and respect, as valued and important individuals, not just another cog in a wheel and you will encourage a culture of cooperation and teamwork. This will help you to successfully complete your objectives every time. This is a lesson/experience, whilst transferable and useful in any organisation, these senior managers have either never learnt or have ignored completely.

Immediately after commissioning, young officers are taught the art of motivating the men and women for whom they have command responsibilities. This involves; discipline matters when necessary, their welfare at all times and being strong leaders in all conditions. To do this, good communication at all times is paramount and every one must know - to the last detail - what is expected of them. To do this, the following is necessary:

- Line management/leadership structure

- Lines of communication to cover the whole structure

- Delegate tasks/responsibilities for every group/team.

- Set realistic targets that include every one.

- Outline in detail, the reporting procedures and time-scales for such reports.

- Set alternative strategies to ensure successful completion.

- Set up meaningful reward systems.

- Identify likely supporters.

It seems to me that the Leeds City Council's Management Team or Leadership Group followed none of the good leadership requirements, which I outlined above because members of staff were making comments such as; "we were left out in the cold", "we did not know what was happening", "we were a department but had no committee to report to", "we were in fact nothing".

The organisation got itself into such horrendous mess because the majority of the staff members are professional people and as professionals; their work ethics, standards of work and effective/efficient management of projects and subordinates are detailed in their respective professional institution's membership requirements. It seems then, that the organisation has given up a lot of its strategic leadership and senior management to the professional institutions. There was no evidence of; proper Planning, Monitoring and Reviews carried out by the Senior Management Team or any other managers.

- Planning – the Management Team should discuss with staff their priorities and objectives for the coming period - say one year -. These objectives should be written down and there should be a discussion of how progress will be monitored.

- Monitoring – the Staff and Manager would keep progress under review throughout the period, taking any supportive action needed.

- Review – Manager and Staff would formally review achievements over the set period and evaluate progress against the objective set.

The exact time scale, after the implementation phase, is an area of debate to which the Senior Management Team could contribute. There is no single answer for all organisations. Much depends on the patterns of workload within the organisation and the availability of data/information, which may be part of the review.

For example, in the case of the Design Engineers, it might seem sensible to hold the reviews after the annual reports have been completed so that the data and other information could be made available.

There is no easy answer to the question of timing of the review period. It does not have to be identical for every team/section. If a manager has a team of four colleagues to review, it would be advisable to space these over a period of time rather than try to do them all in one rush. However, co-ordinating development needs will always be difficult in such a scheme.

Staffing level was reduced to 130. There were people in the department who, due to lack of qualifications were not included in the new structure and for the same reason they were unable to find other jobs. Recruiting qualified staff from outside the organisation filled some vacancies – to overcome skills shortage - in the new structure. Some highly qualified staffs that were included in the new structure left the organisation and took employment with private organisations. This compounded the problem for senior managers because the employees they wanted to keep either left the organisation for other employment or took early retirement, thus leaving employees whom the senior managers wanted to get rid of. The organisation got itself into such a mess with regards getting work done that it had to encourage some of those people who took early retirement to take on some of the work as Private Consultants.

One Engineer said:

> "I am being paid more than twice my usual salary, as a Consultant, for doing the same work and I work from home".

Organisational Culture

Johnson and Scholes [3] argue that:

"The successful implementation of strategic change must take account of the history of the organisation and the dominant values or cultures which exist".

Organisational culture is important in this case because: -

It influences management style

Both culture and management style has a considerable influence on the success or failure of a total quality programme.

Schein [4] suggests that the values of people within an organisation are shaped by such influences as; the history of the organisation, dominant groups within the organisation and their own aspirations and expectations of the organisation.

Dominant groups within the organisation will evolve and legislate to protect and reinforce their values. Formal systems are supported by only condoning those patterns of behaviour, in the formal system that is consistent with the norms of the dominant organisational culture in a certain way. For example; no one could deny that Virgin Airline exhibits a different style to, say, British Airways. Closer examination of the historical development of Virgin Airways reveals the profound influence that the values of Sir Richard Branson have on today's management style.

Arguably, organisational culture is synonymous with management style as the late 80s events at British Leyland, largely attributed to the management style of Michael Edwards, have demonstrated.

Management style will exert an influence over the following key areas:

1. Organisational development

2. Management relationships

3. Industrial relations

4. Successful change implementation

Organisational Structure – Leeds Design Consultancy

STRATEGIC PLANNING	POLITICAL COMMITTEES, DIRECTOR OF TECHNICAL SERVICES, DIRECTOR OF ADMINISTRATION
STRATEGIC PLANNING	ASSISTANT DIRECTORS, CHIEF CITY ARCHITECT
MANAGEMENT PLANNING	CHIEF BUILDING SERVICES ENGINEER, CHIEF ARCHITECT, CHIEF QUANTITY SURVEYOR, CHIEF STRUCTURAL ENGINEER

R. Ashley Rawlins TD. DL.

Structure Before Reorganisation

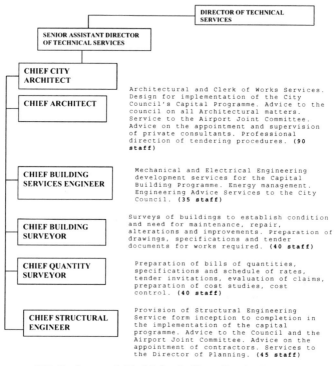

DIRECTOR OF TECHNICAL SERVICES

SENIOR ASSISTANT DIRECTOR OF TECHNICAL SERVICES

CHIEF CITY ARCHITECT

CHIEF ARCHITECT

Architectural and Clerk of Works Services. Design for implementation of the City Council's Capital Programme. Advice to the council on all Architectural matters. Service to the Airport Joint Committee. Advice on the appointment and supervision of private consultants. Professional direction of tendering procedures. **(90 staff)**

CHIEF BUILDING SERVICES ENGINEER

Mechanical and Electrical Engineering development services for the Capital Building Programme. Energy management. Engineering Advice Services to the City Council. **(35 staff)**

CHIEF BUILDING SURVEYOR

Surveys of buildings to establish condition and need for maintenance, repair, alterations and improvements. Preparation of drawings, specifications and tender documents for works required. **(40 staff)**

CHIEF QUANTITY SURVEYOR

Preparation of bills of quantities, specifications and schedule of rates, tender invitations, evaluation of claims, preparation of cost studies, cost control. **(40 staff)**

CHIEF STRUCTURAL ENGINEER

Provision of Structural Engineering Service form inception to completion in the implementation of the capital programme. Advice to the Council and the Airport Joint Committee. Advice on the appointment of contractors. Services to the Director of Planning. **(45 staff)**

250 Members of Staff Including Clerical Support

Structure after Reorganisation

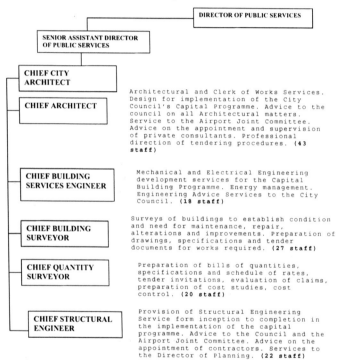

DIRECTOR OF PUBLIC SERVICES

SENIOR ASSISTANT DIRECTOR OF PUBLIC SERVICES

CHIEF CITY ARCHITECT

CHIEF ARCHITECT

Architectural and Clerk of Works Services. Design for implementation of the City Council's Capital Programme. Advice to the council on all Architectural matters. Service to the Airport Joint Committee. Advice on the appointment and supervision of private consultants. Professional direction of tendering procedures. **(43 staff)**

CHIEF BUILDING SERVICES ENGINEER

Mechanical and Electrical Engineering development services for the Capital Building Programme. Energy management. Engineering Advice Services to the City Council. **(18 staff)**

CHIEF BUILDING SURVEYOR

Surveys of buildings to establish condition and need for maintenance, repair, alterations and improvements. Preparation of drawings, specifications and tender documents for works required. **(27 staff)**

CHIEF QUANTITY SURVEYOR

Preparation of bills of quantities, specifications and schedule of rates, tender invitations, evaluation of claims, preparation of cost studies, cost control. **(20 staff)**

CHIEF STRUCTURAL ENGINEER

Provision of Structural Engineering Service form inception to completion in the implementation of the capital programme. Advice to the Council and the Airport Joint Committee. Advice on the appointment of contractors. Services to the Director of Planning. **(22 staff)**

130 Members of Staff Including Clerical Support

The objectives of the Architect's Department at all levels are measurable and although planning is necessary at all levels, care is taken, not to over plan. The Department's main objectives as stated by Senior Management are:

1. Survival of the organisation in competition with private organisations.

2. Improvement in the quality of life for the people of Leeds at no additional cost to the public.

3. Low level of employee turnover, reflecting a good employer.

4. "Internal Peace" or no ulcers for management as this objective is often called.

5. Maximisation of salaries.

The Capital Programme

A review of the structure was carried out, the results of which is shown in the before and after reorganisation structure diagrams. The Director of Administration declared that there will be slimming down of the department and that people who had the opportunity to go elsewhere will be well advised to do so. At this stage, the Architect's Department was formed into the Leeds Design Consultancy (LDC) Group. So there was; restructuring, reduction in staffing level and renaming/re-branding, these changes were all taking place at the same time.

The intention, which brought about these changes was, that the Architect's Department would move a further step towards establishing itself as capable of competing with outside similar groups. The restructuring was really caused by forces external to the department because, each year a forecast is made of the City Council's activities for the following year. In terms of the capital programme, a forecast is made of the likely programme of expenditure for up to three years ahead.

The forecast having been made, it was found that the capital programme was going to be run down seriously. It was going to be inadequate in terms of supporting the numbers of staff employed in that organisation. Central Government was not allowing Local Government to build houses - which is part of the function of the Architect's Department -, and money was going to be severally reduced in other departments also. An exercise was carried out to; estimate the money available in the capital programme, relate that sum to the intended capital expenditure, change that expenditure into fee income and relate that fee income to staffing requirements. According to the retired Head of Building Services Engineers:

"That exercise confirmed what was already known, which was that we were going to be in a lot of trouble with our staffing level. We were not going to be able to attract enough fees to pay the salaries of all the staff employed by us at that time".

At that stage, having seen that there was a discrepancy between the existing staff numbers and the staffing levels required to for the prospective future work, it was necessary to start planning the necessary staffing level reduction. Reduction in terms of early retirements and relocation of staff to other departments within the Leeds City Council. The idea was to get staffing levels to match the funds that were expected from the capital programme.

This financial dilemma was one of the environmental changes driving the need for restructuring. A new structure was produced, after identifying the posts and levels required, which could be supported by the estimated fee income. This process resulted in a number of people within the organisation who could not be placed in the new structure. These displaced staff were called supernumerary, and because the City Council had a policy of no redundancy and because the work was going to tail off - it was not going to finish suddenly -, a gradual change took place to get the number of people working in the department down to the staffing level, which could be supported by the expected fee income.

According to a Senior Architect:

> "The matching of staff to requirements was achieved to a large extent. A lot of people at the senior level sized the opportunity and took early retirement and others, mainly junior staff, were redeployed to other departments".

When some employees were jumping at the chance of redundancy payments, it is easy to see the reasons for others wanting to follow, especially when they saw some people taking the money then continuing to do the same work and being paid a much higher rate than before. But redundancy payments were not available to all employees, especially those who were believed to be hostile to the politicians and senior managers. There were others who, because of their poor skills and lack of qualifications would have had difficulties finding alternative suitable employment. However, some people use the changes in a positive way to their advantage; for example, one employee joined the department after an accident on a site where he was employed as an electrician. He was assessed as being unsuitable for site work due to his injuries, because of his lack of skills he had no place in the restructured department and at age 25 years, redundancy was not an option. He was interviewed by other City Council's departments but was found to be unsuitable for their existing vacancies. He was encouraged by the department to undertake new skills training, which they supported financially. I interviewed him a number of years later during my research for this book and found that he was a qualified primary school teacher.

Taking redundancy could be the right decision, depending on; your personality, your qualifications, and your skills. You can find out if it is right for you by carrying out a self-analysis. Ask yourself how satisfied you are with your current position. Do you love your job or are you bored or frustrated? If restructuring, the TQM programme and Performance Related Pay (PRP) had not been implemented, would you have been thinking of leaving anyway? If you are happy in your work, then explore how your role might change in the new structure and whether your future in the organisation would improve. If colleagues around you are opting for redundancy, they are likely to justify their decision by being negative about the future prospects of the organisation. But it is not automatic that things will be worse. The changes are meant to improve conditions, so it is worth considering if you can adapt to change readily and could you be enthusiastic about your chances in the restructured organisation.

Mintzberg [5] argues that an organisation's environment shapes organisational form. Certainly, Leeds City Council's environment was, prior to the 1980s, relatively stable compared to the very unstable environment of the late 80s, the 90s and even more so today in mid 2000s. This volatile and continuous change in an organisation's environment tends to encourage a mechanistic management style. Mechanistic describes a management system, which is subject to restrictions and is authoritative in nature. Decision-making was relatively centralised and concentrated on the internal problems of the organisation. However, this pre-occupation with internal issues can become problematic when faced with the type of environmental changes that Leeds City Council and other Local Authority organisations had to face.

Barriers to a Total Quality Programme

Clearly, the scenario I have painted is totally at variance with the underlying concept of total quality management. Management's view of human behaviour was what McGregor would describe as "Theory X".

When an organisation misconducts itself, senior managers may be embarrassed, but other members of staff will be ruined, therefore, they have a right, at least to occupy a position, which will enable them to insist that waste should be eliminated, existing working methods reviewed and changed if out-of-date, and if desirable reorganisation should be carried out. In the City Council, both staff and the general public will suffer when its departments are antiquated and inefficient. Both will want to see that the necessary measures to modernise the organisation are carried out promptly.

For a total quality programme to be successful, a supportive management style is required. The management style adopted by the Leeds City Council could hardly be described as supportive, at best it was autocratic. Decision-making was centralised, systems and procedures were formalised to the extent that they were; cumbersome, and slow to respond to problems at the "grass roots" of the organisation.

Unlike Japanese companies where total quality management had evolved, there was no harmonious relationship between employees and the organisation. Employees begrudged doing more than they had to, either because of lack of commitment or because they believed that they would not be rewarded.

The Current organisational structure for the Architect's Department, comprising line management and support functions seems to be less than effective. Any evaluation of the organisation's structure and detailed roles needs to be based on the premise: will it meet the requirements of Leeds City Council and the public as outlined later in the "Organisational Structure for Leeds City Council"? The areas of suggested change are intended to accurately reflect environmental changes, for example; Central Government legislations as well as to facilitate an appropriate and relevant contribution being made by members of staff throughout the organisation. If the organisation is to compete effective with similar but private organisations then its structure needs to be both dynamic and designed to tap the relative potential of its entire staff.

Motives and values can be ascribed directly to individuals but not to organisations. We can sometimes explain the behaviour of an organisation in purely situational terms, for example; by consideration of its tasks, resources and the nature of its environment, but these explanations tend to be particular and partial, and requires reference to individual evaluations as well as to organisational needs. The behaviour of a Local Authority organisation is usually only understood in terms of aims and values of its social groups. These groups will often be formally organised also, for example; as a pressure group or as a professional body. The social groups in question may be external to the organisation or occupy an internal position of either a political or professional character or they can sometimes occupy both positions.

There was little or no involvement of members of staff - below the level of Operational Planning - in the decision-making process, and a great deal of alienation existed between different levels of staff within the organisation. This was particularly noticeable at the levels occupied by Junior Design Engineers and Inspectors, where this behaviour prevented meaningful working relationships developing with their first line supervisors. Consequently, there was little or no joint effort towards achieving the organisation's goals/targets. The whole organisation was so wrapped up in its internal domestic problems that there was a distinct lack of sensitivity to and awareness of the external environment and its changes.

We all have belief systems we live by, which are deeply connected to our values. We are motivated by and make decisions based on those belief systems and values – often subconsciously -. If we all had the same values with the same priorities, making decisions on organisational change would be simple – but we don't -. Our lives are unique because our values and beliefs are formed through different routes and through individual experiences. There, to attempt to change other people's values and beliefs through force, manipulation or ridicule is pointless and counterproductive. If our values conflict when making a decision, the values with the highest priority will decide the outcome of that decision-making process. For example; if completing a report is of greater importance to an employee than keeping a meeting appointment, that employee – although normally punctual – will continue to work on the report and either be late for the appointment or not attend the meeting.

We communicate our values; with almost every sentence we speak, in what we choose to talk about and in what we complain about to anyone who is tuned in to listen. Knowing and acknowledging other people's hierarchy of values gives you the opportunity to influence or persuade them, because you have respected and accommodated their value system.

Use the following table to compare your hierarchy of values with your colleagues and other employees:

Table for Hierarchy of Values	
CORE VALUES	**PRIORITY (1-18)** **(1=high)(18=low)**
REPUTATION	
SELF-RESPECT	
MY CHILDREN'S RESPECT	
MONEY	
FAMILY	
LOVE	
LOYALTY	
RELIGION	
INDEPENDENCE	
FUN	
HONESTY	
SUCCESS	
MANNERS	
PERSONAL HONOUR	
STATUS	
LAUGHTER	
ETHICS	
INTEGRITY	

Another barrier to the successful implementation of a total quality programme existed in the Architects Department's existing systems. Far from being a fertile ground from which total quality could evolve, quality control was executed through a network of projects inspectors and quality controllers. This had the effect of taking the responsibility for total quality away from the first line managers/supervisors. This was unlike the "total quality" concept as operated by Japanese organisations, where individuals and supervisors were encouraged to pass their quality problems to a quality control section. The situation at Leeds City Council Architect's Department was hardly likely to lead to a "push upwards" from the supervisors in the direction of total quality management, which was the case in Japan.

Nottingham City Council, where a TQM programme was successfully implemented during 1992/93, first installed quality systems and quality centres, and had the "quality mark" and "investors in people" before embarking on the TQM programme for the entire City Council.

With Leeds City Council, on the other hand, there was a considerable miss-match between the existing organisational culture and what was considered necessary to support a successful TQM programme implementation. So why did Leeds City Council thought that it could introduce a TQM programme into such a hostile environment and make it work? When people work together, they establish social relationships and customary ways of doing things, and this is the pattern of behaviour that gets established. How people work together in practice cannot be laid down in any job descriptions, because it will depend upon; the relations that develop between people, the kind of people they are, their particular strengths and weaknesses and how they react to each other. Different social groups will develop within the organisation and these groups will influence the attitudes and actions of their members. What tends to happen in these social groups is that they may develop informal methods of getting their work done. This can have important effects on organisational efficiency. For example; at the Rover Group, - a motor car manufacturer located in the Midlands, England - a "Quality Circle" was formed, in the early 1990s, to look at areas where poor quality was identified and was affecting efficiency and output. Their remit was to discuss the problems with managers and between them find a solution. One problem identified was that bolts from a certain manufacturer did not meet the specification. Rather than informing the bolt manufacturer that their bolts cannot be used because they did not meet the specification, the "Quality Circle" group from Rover, spent a number of days with the bolts manufacturer showing them how to manufacturer bolts. The question I asked the Finance Director of Rover Group, who at that moment was singing the praises of these employees, was; who was manufacturing the motorcars when these employees were away manufacturing bolts? His reply was that they were happy, it made them feel good, and they were more committed to the organisation. The Rover Group collapsed and went out of business in 2004.

Leeds City Council's organisational structure

Leeds City Council employs about 32,000 people. The organisation is made up of seven departments - listed below -, five of which deliver nearly 500 specialist services to its customers, and two that provide corporate and strategic support services.

With the exception of the Chief Executive's Department, each council department has a director who is ultimately responsible for ensuring that their department delivers on the priorities outlined for their services in the latest Council Plan. They are supported by a departmental management team, made up of chief officers who are responsible for the individual services that make up their department. These departments and their responsibilities are outlined below:

Chief Executive's Department - Provides a specific range of corporate and strategic services to the council, includi ng; legal and democratic services, procurement, customer services, the Public Private Partnership unit and executive support services such as communications and equality. The Department also includes; Leeds Initiative, the city's local strategic partnership, the Connexions West Yorkshire. The Director of Children's Services, also sit within the Chief Executive's Department.

City Services Department - Nine divisions deliver; environmental enforcement, highways, catering and cleaning, buildings and facilities management, and transportation services.

Corporate Services Department - Seven divisions deliver; financial, audit, human resources and information communication technology (ICT) related services to the council.

Development Department - Delivers services in six key areas, including; asset management, design services, economic services, planning and development services, and strategy and policy.

Learning and Leisure Department - Eight divisions deliver services, including; arts and heritage, libraries, parks and countryside, sport and active recreation, early years, jobs and skills and youth support.

Neighbourhoods and Housing Department - Provides services in; community safety, environmental health, area management, property management, as well as strategic housing services.

Social Services Department - Delivers social care services based around the specific needs of children and adults. Both adult and children's service areas contain specialist service areas but in general, Social Services aims to support people to live as independently and as safely as possible in their own homes and communities.

Responsibility for managing homes owned by Leeds City Council is held by six organisations, which are separate from the council, known as arms length management organisations (ALMOs). Each housing ALMO is responsible for council-owned homes in one particular area of Leeds.

The Architect's Department is also an arms length management organisation (ALMO) and provides a consultancy service to all Leeds City Council's departments and areas for all of their Building and Engineering works.

In addition, local authority education services in Leeds are managed by **Education Leeds**, a not-for-profit company, wholly owned by Leeds City Council. The company was established in April 2001 and is a unique partnership between the council and private sector support service company.

The city's strategic partnership group, the Leeds Initiative, is also based within the council, although it brings together a range of partners from the public, private, community and voluntary sectors.

Corporate Policy Guidance

It is the custom of the City Treasurer to issue an annual statement in August - September of each year, setting out the global budget guidance for the forthcoming year. This statement is generally considered extremely useful. It sets the financial climate for the coming year; informs/guides managers on anticipated growth or reduction in spending.

The City Treasurer's statement is intended to provide guidance on corporate priorities in respect of the revenue budget. It also suggests a method for identifying strategic service priorities and detailed guidance, which will be issued in September of each year.

The primary purpose of this budget preparation/prediction, is to hasten the transition from a "finance-led" to a "policy and priority-led" annual revenue budget. Accordingly, it will be for Committee Members to determine the City Council's corporate and strategic service priorities before the process of preparing Service Plans and proposing detailed resource allocation begins.

Once the service priorities have been determined, these priorities are used to establish clear criteria by which Council Members may make both strategic and specific choices between competing demands for the limited resources that are available.

I spoke with the present head of the Architect's Department or LDC in April 2006 – who was a Junior Manager / Architect when I left that department in March 1990 – and he said:

> "We have gone through so many changes since you left, name changes, location

> changes, partnerships with other departments and private organisations. I consider myself an expert in Change Management and we are doing well. I am proposing that I take the lead in rolling out this process throughout the City Council. The organisation as a whole has an annual budget in excess of £2 billion and each year it is spent inefficiently. That is my view but other senior managers agree with me and I am sure that a high percentage of the tax-paying public are concerned about inefficiencies too. There is no proper prioritisation of resources. At the moment, resources are allocated on the basis of he who shouts the loudest gets the most and that is no good for the public. I want to take the lead in changing that process to give the public better value for their money".

His statement came as a shock to me because I could not understand why an Officer of the Leeds City Council feel that he/she has the right or the authority to make such policy decisions as the priorities of community projects. They - City Council Officers - are not elected members and I am certain that members of the public would be just as surprise as I was to learn that their communities' priorities were decided by officers and not elected members.

He also said:

> "We have formed a partnership called The Strategic Design Alliance. This partnership will deliver the very best architectural services for the future development

across the city. In July 2006 the Council's Architectural Design Services and Jacobs Consultants formed an alliance that combines high levels of public and private consultancy experience, at the same time, enhancing capacity and responsiveness".

However, some of the recent partnerships with private organisations seem to be having some success. In August 2007, it was reported that the Leeds City Council's in-house architectural group, The Strategic Design Alliance, were the leaders in the ground-breaking design concepts – of two schools in inner city Leeds and a library in Otley – that won eight highly acclaimed national and regional awards for their work on those new buildings. The awards highlight how the buildings have been designed to meet the needs of the local communities as well as enhance and improve the local areas.

My investigation into this matter highlighted a much more disturbing situation. In the mid 1990s Leeds City Council Failed a general inspection and one of the major areas of concern was the lack of strategic leadership by the elected members. It stated that elected members did not spend enough time with the organisation in dealing with strategic decision-making. The ruling group at that time restructured the Members' Committee out of which came the Executive Board. Each executive board member has responsibility for a department - as outlined in the City Council Structure - and for this responsibility, they are being paid a salary. This is in contrast to the idea that an elected member of the local authority was providing a voluntary service to his/her community. In addition to this, some of these elected members have no management qualifications or management experience and so is dependent on officers to help them with that function. Some unscrupulous officers are using this state of affaires to dominate elected members and in so doing are making strategic decisions on behalf of elected members.

Comprehensive Performance Assessment

Leeds has been judged as one of the highest performing authorities in the country and is considered to be improving well. With budgets of around £2 billion, serving a population of approximately three quarters of a million people, the council is the largest single tier authority in the country to be awarded "four stars" in the year 2005 Comprehensive Performance Assessment (CPA), the highest rating available.

Each year, the council is measured on how well it is delivering and improving services to local people and their communities and in the year 2005 there have been significant changes to the assessment process. The assessment is now much harder and the test is more stringent. The assessment now uses a system of stars to indicate overall performance, and judges how well the council has improved since the previous year's assessment, with a direction of travel statement.

All council services are assessed each year through the CPA framework. The assessment concluded that; the council has a sound track record in improving its priority services and achieving improved outcomes for residents, especially those from the more disadvantaged communities.

Delegated Decisions

Specified officers of the Council may take a range of decisions, known as delegated decisions, without reference to a Board or Committee meeting of Elected Members. All delegated decisions are recorded and will have a written report and background papers available in support of such a decision and are subject to 'call-in' by one of the council's Scrutiny Boards.

Key decisions are included in the forward plan which the Council publishes each month - over £500,000 in value or affecting 2 or more wards -.

Major decisions are not in the forward plan - over £100,000 in value or affecting 1 or more wards -.

Area Committees

Area Committees give the public the opportunity to have more influence on how services are delivered to their area. The Area Committee aims to; improve the delivery and co-ordination of local council services, and improve the quality of local decision-making. Area Committees give local people a local way of addressing their local priorities.

Leeds City Council has divided the city into 5 areas or "wedges". Each wedge has an "inner" and an "outer" Area Committee. The committee is made up of the councillors who are elected in an area to represent the views of the people in that area.

Area Committees are responsible for making sure that good quality services are being delivered as required in that area. To do this, they have to find out what people think are the priorities for their area and turning them into a local action plan called an Area Delivery Plan. Area Committees are expected to report regularly, how they are doing against their Delivery Plan to make a difference and meet the priorities.

Area Committees have a lot of influence; they are to make sure that local priorities are taken into account in the development of major policies and strategies.

As a result of past consultation, each Area Committee is initially concentrating on improving council services in the following areas:

- Street scene - keeping the streets clean, emptying bins, maintaining roads and grassy areas.

- Youth Service - providing activities and support for young people.

- Community Safety - helping to make the community/ area safer through the presence of; Neighbourhoods and Street Wardens, Police Community Support Officers, CCTV schemes, preventing burglaries

The Area Committees are also responsible for making sure that different organisations work together better so that their priorities are addressed. To do this, a District Partnership has been set up in each wedge. These District Partnerships are made up of major organisations that deliver key services to the area such as; the Primary Care Trust, the Police, local companies, voluntary and community groups and Leeds City Council. The District Partnerships come under the umbrella of the Leeds Initiative - a citywide partnership made up from the major organisations in the city. Each wedge has an area manager who is leading on the delivery of the area's local priorities.

Area Delivery Plans

These plans have been developed with the assistance of Council Departments and partner agencies, which operate within each Area Management District.

The purposes of Area Delivery Plans are; to guide the work of the Area Committees over the coming year, setting out service priorities and improvement strategies for each area. The plans also provide a mechanism for directing resources and a framework for investing well-being budgets in each of the areas.

Consultation and communication

A Member of Leeds City Council's Executive Committee said:

> "Leeds City Council takes its obligation to consult with all service users across the city very seriously. We listen to what you think about our services so that we know what needs to be improved and what people are happy with.
>
> In our Council Plan we have committed ourselves to making big improvements in the way we consult with the people of Leeds. This includes the following:

- Developing a consistent approach.

- Improved planning for consultations.

- Better communication on the impact and results of consultations.

- Managing consultation processes more effectively.

- Providing more information on the issues relating to consultation.

  We use a number of different methods of consultation. These include; both small and large-scale surveys, forums, focus groups and market research. We contract specialist market research organisations for large-scale surveys to make sure our consultations are effective.

  We consult with; residents, specific service users, businesses, user groups - such as disabled people or ethnic minority groups -, local area groups, individual local communities or various third party and representative bodies. Greater diversity across the range of groups that we consult with means that we can gather more information to help influence our decisions and developments more appropriately.

  Every three years, we carry out a major survey covering every aspect of the council's services. This is called the Best Value General Survey and the last one was carried out in 2006."

Background to Corporate Governance

The term "Corporate Governance" came into common use in the UK, in a company context, in 1992. Since then, it has been widely used in both the private sector and public services. Corporate Governance is the system by which organisations are directed and controlled.

According to the Independent Commission on Good Governance in Public Services, there are six core principles of good governance:

1. Good governance means focussing on the organisation's purpose and outcomes for citizens and service users.

2. Good governance means performing effectively in clearly defined functions and roles.

3. Good governance means promoting values for the whole organisation and demonstrating the values of good governance through behaviour.

4. Good governance means taking informed, transparent decisions and managing risk.

5. Good governance means developing the capacity and capability of the governing body to be effective.

6. Good governance means engaging stakeholders and making accountability real.

Customer satisfaction monitoring

Leeds City Council is firmly committed to carrying out market research and consultation proactively across all our services and functions. They believe that the best way of finding out what people think about a service is quite simply to ask them.

In recent years, Leeds City Council have developed a coordinated approach to consultation, with; forward planning, better sharing information across the council and improved quality and effectiveness of surveys. Most importantly, they have made it a priority to take positive action from customer feedback and the results of any surveys that are carried out.

Measuring customer satisfaction helps the City Council to understand where and how to improve its services. This is important, as the Council needs to know which services customers feel are successful and which may need a change of focus. One of the functions of the council's Customer First Board is, amongst other things, to regularly review progress in these areas.

One of the main indicators of how the council is performing is the Best Value General Survey - a survey carried out by all local authorities in the country every three years, under the guidance of the Office of the Deputy Prime Minister. The survey measures levels of general customer satisfaction both as a whole and in specific areas such as; waste and recycling, sports and recreational facilities, and museums and galleries.

The results of the 2003 Best Value General Survey for Leeds City Council were released in March 2004 and were very encouraging. The survey showed that the Council achieved a 5% increase - to 77% - in general customer satisfaction with the services of the council, since the survey carried out in 2000. Leeds City Council bucks the downward trends of 10% decreases nationally and 7% regionally.

The next Best Value General Survey was carried out in October 2006, but the results were not made available in time for inclusion in this book.

Leeds Annual Survey

The Leeds Annual Survey is very specific to Leeds and will be carried out every year. From 2006 onwards the research will be carried out in July and August with the publication of the results due towards the end of the year. The inaugural survey in 2005 was carried out in September and October with the raw data being available in December and the results available in 2006. Surveying residents every year will enable the council to assess continuous improvement. The survey aim to provide a new internal benchmark for assessing satisfaction in areas such as; quality of life, year-on-year service delivery performance, priorities for budget considerations and communicating with residents effectively. Future surveys will enable the council to build a picture of the trends in service delivery in these very specific categories.

The survey is believed to be the most comprehensive and high profile survey carried out across the council each year with 2,000 residents being surveyed each year. Sampling is carefully carried out so that it isn't just the 'usual suspects' or a large volume of the same type of respondents. The 2,000 samples are stratified so that there is a breakdown of people in each area management 'wedge' being consulted.

The sample, as a "snapshot", is representative of the city's population in terms of gender, ethnicity, age and geographic locations. The method used is face-to-face as this is a very productive mans of extracting interesting and useful views.

The survey is expected to help Leeds City Council to demonstrate, both; a more co-ordinated approach to surveying a broad range of people and how it can rationalise the volume of smaller broad satisfaction surveys, in order to help maintain its status through the Comprehensive Performance Assessment review. Comprehensive, up-to-date council-wide information has been made available to all departments. It is important that the council, as an organisation, measure its progress in terms of continuous improvement on a regular basis.

The survey is also expected to accommodate the performance areas that the City Council need to measure more consistently, for example; best value, quality of life, service delivery and communicating with citizens effectively. The sample of 2,000 has a significantly greater range than any individual departmental surveys could realise and can be broken down into data ranges.

Due to the size and scope of the survey - and nature of the research needed, an external consultant is being used. This will also demonstrate that the surveying is being carried out independently. The consultant is responsible for supplying the experienced and trained fieldwork researchers to survey residents on a face-to-face basis in their homes so that views are gathered, out in their own communities.

The survey asks residents about their overall perceptions in subject areas such as:

- Overall satisfaction with the council and how it runs things.

- Whether services have improved, stayed the same or worsened.

- Quality of life in the area and satisfaction with local neighbourhoods.

- Levels of respect for citizens and their communities.

- Priorities to consider when budget setting.

- Service delivery satisfaction – front line services.

- Satisfaction with facilities and events.

- Enforcement.

- Transport.

- Access to services.

- Means of communicating with residents.

- Access to information and technology.

The layout, answer options and question style are similar to the General Survey for consistency purposes.

The surveying is carried out on a face-to-face basis as this method enables the council to really explore what people think.

The results of surveys are made available to; staff, managers, directors, and the media and, of course, the citizens of Leeds.

Residents are usually contacted at random and then encouraged to participate if they haven't been surveyed before. The sample is strictly controlled to ensure that the City Council get a broad mix of views.

Service departments are using the survey results as an indication of levels of customer satisfaction. The information can be used for; planning, service improvement, profile raising, citizen engagement and benchmarking purposes. Data will also be available to compare and contrast on a "wedge" basis to help focus upon service priorities.

Carrying out the survey on a corporate basis will enable the City Council to compare and contrast statistics right across the council. The survey is based upon corporate priorities for the council rather than taking each department's subject areas in isolation. The survey process is project managed by a cross-departmental management board that ensures input from all departments.

The Annual Survey represents the council's most comprehensive sample of; data, statistics and information from residents. It will rationalise some of the ad hoc general satisfaction surveys carried out by departments, by allowing them to spend their time carrying out much more specific service user research. This survey is high profile and the results are quite significant in terms of service delivery.

The survey should reduce the volume of small, ad hoc general satisfaction surveys that go out individually and replace them with one key survey that aims to consult with residents not usually surveyed. The survey takes place at the same time every year, allowing other consultations to be planned accordingly. Some data from the annual survey can replace other data thus removing the need to carry out some - but not all - "additional" consultations.

The survey aims to survey 2,000 people each year who have not taken part in major surveys before. The consultants carrying out the survey have been tasked with ensuring that a proportion of the sample of 2,000 people come from communities that do not feature in other surveys regularly enough. The consultants must ensure that the City Council "reach out" to these citizens and find out their views.

Proposed Corporate Strategies

In planning services and allocating resources, the following corporate objectives are regarded as priorities:

- To implement the City Council's "Charter for Leeds" objectives.

- To ensure that services are delivered in accordance with the Council's core values on; a) marketing, quality and customer care; b) effectiveness, efficiency and economy; c) protecting the environment; d) tackling inequality and disadvantage; e) staff care, motivation and development.

- To implement the "Leeds into the 90s and beyond" programme for improving the quality of the City Council's services.

- To continue the economic regeneration of the City of Leeds.

- To prepare the ground for success, when the time comes to compete for contracts with regards new service areas, subject to Central Government Compulsory Competitive Tendering (CCT) legislation.

- To enhance the Leeds City's prospects as a Regional European Capital.

- To promote safety within the Leeds City's different communities and tackle the fear of crime.

- To develop and implement a health and anti-poverty strategy for the City of Leeds.

- To implement the Central Government's Citizens' Charter legislation.

Identifying Strategic Service Priorities

A senior councillor and member of the Executive Board argued that the City Council's main service priorities are:

- "A clear sense of purpose and direction in this respect is every bit as essential as setting overall corporate goals. In order that these priorities be determined by Elected Members - not officers - and in sufficient time to influence and direct the preparation of service plans and budgets.

- That in early August, Chief Officers are requested to propose strategic priorities for the major service blocks within their departments. These priorities are based on the following; a) corporate goals as set out above and the treasurer's global budgetary guidance; b) anticipated Member aims as derived from Committee reports and the Council's Charter for Leeds; c) issues, trends and legislations likely to impact on services within their departments.

- That by early September, an "Issues and Priorities" paper, bringing together the corporate and service dimensions, is prepared by the Chief Executive for consideration at a meeting of Chairs and Vice Chairs - elected members - in the middle of that month.

- That the resolution of members on corporate and strategic service priorities is immediately issued to Planning and Operational Managers as guidance in their planning of services and preparation of the annual revenue budget."

Summary of Key Points

In this part of the book I have tried to draw out a number of key points from a very complicated situation.

The City Council's management style and organisational culture were, and still are to a large extent, at variance with the total quality management concept, although senior managers are now talking in terms of change management and not total quality management.

Before selecting the consultants to advice on the TQM programme the decision-makers did not develop a clear business case for the programme. In selecting the consultants the decision-makers took into account only application and methodologies, ignoring adaptability and freshness. There were no engagements with staff at all levels; only decision-makers were involved. Communication with stakeholders - the community and other City Council's client departments - was non-existent. The consultants' experience to deliver such a programme was questionable. The majority of people involved in the project - including client departments - felt that they would not benefit from the programme and there were no attempts by the decision-makers to alleviate this pessimism. Although the consultants and decision-makers appear to work together, I do not feel that value was delivered. In addition to the lack of clarity about the TQM programme, all employees did not have a proper understanding of the consultants' role and a high proportion became frustrated about what was expected. Client departments and the community had no input into the planning or implementation of the programme but had to deal with the consequences of the lack of confidence in the consultants.

If an organisation gets its internal communications right, it will find itself with a very powerful tool that will drive up motivation and productivity because, well-informed staff are usually more committed to organisational achievements. Good communications could help organisations retain their best members of staff and it does not necessarily have to be very expensive financially or otherwise. However, it requires some lateral thinking by strategic and planning managers and lateral thinking managers seems to be very scarce.

Barriers existed within the organisation that could not be overcome by the introduction of a total quality management programme, for example; the "us and them" attitude. The organisation would have had better success with the implementation of the TQM programme if it had spent some time and effort in changing the culture of the organisation before introducing TQM. Without a change in organisational culture nothing else will change and the environment will not be conducive to change and the introduction of TQM will fail. When people work together, they; develop social relationships and common ways of doing things and certain patterns of behaviour gets established. How people work together cannot be laid down in the job description or person specification, no matter how compressively they are written, because it will depend upon; the relations that develop between staff, on the kind of people they are, their particular strengths and weaknesses and how they interact with each other. Organisations are not just a collection of individuals performing specific functions of the jobs allocated to them. Organisations are also; sets of social relations made up of how one individual reacts with another to influence the attitudes and actions of members of their groups.

Over 70% of the employees of LDC and other client departments with whom I spoke felt that the reason for them not being consulted was due to lack of respect by decision-makers and the consultants. Some employees went further and stated that; "we suffered more than lack of respect, our jobs and activities were changed for no good reason, we were denied any opportunities to take part in discussions in changes to situations and conditions that directly affected us, we were not valued as persons or citizens". One employee said; "in effect, that denial of opportunities to participate in something that affected us directly, interfered with our freedom and there were no justifications for it". Mathew Arnold [6] arguing about this lack of respect and opportunities, claimed that; "for the common bulk of mankind, to live in a society of equals tends in general to make a man's sprits expand, and his faculties work easily and actively; while, to live in a society of superiors, although it may occasionally be very good and discipline, yet in general tends to tame the sprits and to make the play of the faculties less secure and active". R. H. Tawney [7] made similar assumptions, arguing that; "individuals differ profoundly in capacity and character but they are equally entitled, as human beings, to consideration and respect. The well-being of a society is likely to be increased if it so plans its organisation that, whether their powers are great or small, all its members may be equally enabled to make the best of such powers as they possess". Freedom for the strong is oppression for the weak. When steps are taken to reduce inequality, it will be seen by some people as infringement of their freedom, and we must then ask; freedom for whom? There is no such thing as freedom in the abstract. Freedom cannot be divorced from the realities of a particular time and place. It involves a power of choice between alternatives. It means the ability to do, or to refrain from doing, definite things, at a definite moment, in definite circumstances, or it mean nothing at all. Tawney [8] argues that if freedom is used negatively then liberty and equality are condemned to be foes, but if freedom is used in a positive way and everyone benefits from its use then liberty and equality can live as friends.

Some attempts were made to change the environment into which total quality was introduced. Unfortunately this occurred simultaneously with the introduction of the total quality programme. Social climate includes all the social factors that affect the way people behave. When we look at why managers take certain actions, we will find that their particular environment influences many of them. This will show up in the way in which managers and staff, in a professional organisation, behave towards other people within the organisation and the decisions that they take. How managers treat; their junior staff, each other and clients/customers, will depend not only on their character, but more on what is customary at that time in their organisation, locality and country. It is said in some change management programmes that "If you want to change the people – change the people". This is something that organisations should take on board when considering the introduction of a TQM programme. The above quotation is about changing the attitudes of your people, so that, you could release the potential in your organisation for the successful implementation of organisational change. Successful TQM programmes require successful change management programmes. The problems faced by the department have solutions, but the Strategic Managers seems to be treating other employees as if they were genetically programmed machines. What distinguishes humans from other animals is their social existence and their capacity, under certain conditions to transform their own organisations and hence their own mode of working to create efficient organisations. The Strategic Managers should have used this knowledge to mobilise this very creative group of employees to transform the problems into solutions, instead of creating a situation where a high percentage of that group of creative employees felt alienated and not respected.

The feasibility study was unrealistic in its assessment of the concept and the outcome of introducing the total quality management programme into a single department of a local authority organisation. The feasibility study ignored changes in the external environment that would impact on the whole of Leeds City Council. It concentrated on the single department and although that department was larger than most medium sized organisations the changes taking place in other City Council's departments, and in the environment external to Leeds City Council, would have a major impact on the way the Architect's Department is organised and managed. Around the time that the feasibility study was conducted, it was fashionable to decry Central Government's performance as a total disaster in, which the success are forgotten and only the failures are remembered. There were failures in some economic policies, for example; unemployment was high, inflation was increasing and economic growth was slowing. Over a period of time growth was sacrificed to the balance of payments despite the revenue from North Sea Oil, for example; the fixed and unrealistic rate of exchange. Central Government constrained public expenditure on which so much else depended. This upset and antagonised the Trade Unions, alienated large groups of workers, derailed the National Plan and frustrated policies for improving the industrial structure. The distribution of income saw dramatic changes due to the decrease in the share of profits in GDP and increase in the share of wages and salaries. Changes related to benefits resulted in large increases in government social expenditure. Reforms were implemented nationally, for example; the reorganisation of government, the attack on environmental pollution, the impetus to regional land-use planning, encouragement of the conservation of both historic cities and the countryside, many libertarian reforms coming on to the statute book by the Home Secretary.

The objectives that were set for the total quality programme were far too ambitious given the limited influence of a single department on Leeds City Council as a whole. As stated earlier, there were too many changes taking place within the organisation and externally that also affected the organisation and any attempts to introduce a total quality programme at that stage was unlikely to be successful. Besides the changes described earlier, there were other changes taking place, which also had a major impact on the results of the total quality management implementation. For example; the Architect's Department, in addition to providing the consultancy and project management services for all other Leeds City Council's departments also provided building and engineering maintenance services for the Departments of Housing, Education, Transport, Social Services, Training and City Centre Management. A decision was taken that each of these departments would have its own maintenance section. This caused further problems for the Architect's Department because, not only was it going to lose that part of its department, people were not going to be transferred enblock to the other departments. Further more, because some of these employees were hostile to the Politicians and did not cooperate in some earlier changes then the politicians ware not going to do them any favours. The other departments decided that the jobs in the new sections would be advertised and existing staff should apply for those jobs in competition with external applicants, further more, the jobs were not ring-fenced and existing staffs that were nearing retirement were not short-listed. This created a dilemma for the Architect's Department because at the time when it was required to re-launch itself as a super efficient department in readiness to compete with external organisations, it was left with a number of employees who could not be transferred or redeployed and who had no place in the new department - Leeds Design Consultancy -. The best way to deal with this would have been to offer these people an early retirement package but the politicians turned this idea down because they wanted to make life difficult for this group of workers who were very hostile to them in the pass. These people continued to attend work but day after day they did nothing except when they were bored they would offer to do errands for other staff.

Programme dimensions were not thought through; therefore, it could not be used as a measure of performance. Yet Performance Related Pay (PRP) scheme was developed at the same time as the introduction of the TQM programme. For many years I have been accustomed to organisations having annual performance reviews but they were linked to staff personal development and promotion and not to pay. I was surprised to learn that Leeds City Council and other local authority employees did not have annual performance reviews. I was even more surprised when employees in Leeds Design Consultancy -the Architect's Department - became very hostile to the introduction of annual performance reviews in the form of Performance Related Pay (PRP) Appraisal linked to PRP is accepted as a normal part of everyday business and professional life and if Leeds Design Consultancy (LDC) were to compete with those organisations, it had to fall in line. The union argued that the pay increase available through PRP was too small to act as an incentive, further more that it was demeaning to a professional person to be judged in this way. However, senior managers - myself included - and the quality programme advisors argued that it was a necessary component of the quality programme. It was also noted that some new entrants came into the organisation from a business background because they wanted to escape this competitive element that was inherent in their previous employment. It was argued that since LDC was expected to compete with private organisations for the work it did, it would benefit from a more business-like approach. This is where, with my wider experience gained in other more commercial organisations, I was able to make a useful contribution to the discussions. Some critics of the proposals argue that it will be another two years before the data collection is sufficiently established to allow judgments at individual employee level to be made. In other words, whatever the rights and wrongs of appraisal and PRP, in principle, the organisation is simply moving too fast.

A pilot study approach would have safeguarded the organisation against programme failure. However, this approach was not adopted. No attempts were made to visit or review other organisations that had introduced/implemented a TQM programme. No checks were made to learn if the consultants who were giving advice and training had success with any other organisations.

Most of the above points are reflections, more on the Strategic and Planning Managers ability to understand and recognise the dynamics of the "real" situation that exists within the organisations, rather than on the Total Quality Management programme to produce the goods, in terms of quality and efficiency – achieving the aims and objectives set as a measure of programme success.

Performance Assessment

The criteria used by the organisation for assessing staff, in respect of the Performance Related Pay scheme are as follows:

For Professional Support Staff

Services

> Skills in Organisation.
> Methodology.
> Presentation.
> Reporting Skills.

Technical

> Maintenance/Upgrading of Administrative
> Procedures.
> Problem Analysis.

Personnel, Payroll Knowledge and Administration.
Financial – Planning, Forecasting, Monitoring and Implementation.
Network – Supervision, Maintenance and Development.
Hardware and Software Maintenance and Enhancement.
Computer Skills.

Performance

Productivity - in all functions -.
Business Awareness.
Reliability.
Response to Pressure.
Resourcefulness.
Thoroughness.

Relationships

Communications.
Teamwork.
Personal Contact Skills and Diplomacy.
Relationships with Contractors, Consultants and Suppliers.
Client Confidence.
Leadership and motivation Skills.
Delegation.

Personality

Initiative.
Flair and Original Thought.
Determination and Commitment.

Flexibility.
Attitude to Training.

For Project Coordinators and Senior Professionals

Service

Skills in Organisation.
Methodology.
Presentation.
Reporting Skills.

Technical

Problem analysis.
Financial Appraisal.
Computer Skills.

Performance

Productivity - in all functions -.
Business Awareness.
Reliability.
Response to Pressure.
Resourcefulness.
Thoroughness.

Relationships

Communications.
Teamwork.
Personal Contact Skills and Diplomacy.
Client Confidence.

Leadership.
Delegation.

Personality

Initiative.
Flair and Original Thought.
Determination and Commitment.
Flexibility.
Attitude to Training.

For Structural Engineering, Electrical Engineering, Mechanical Engineering and Architectural Staff.

Design

Design Skills.
Presentation Skills.

Service

Skills in Organisation.
Methodology.
Presentation
Reporting Skills.

Technical

Problem Analysis.
Technical Knowledge.
Contract Knowledge and Administration.
Financial Appraisal.
Computer Skills.

Specification Writing.

Performance

Productivity - in all functions -.
Business Awareness.
Reliability.
Response to Pressure.
Resourcefulness.
Thoroughness.

Relationships

Communications.
Teamwork.
Personal Contact Skills and Diplomacy.
Relationship with Contractors and Consultants.
Client Confidence.
Leadership.
Delegation.

Personality

Initiative.
Flair and Original Thought.
Determination and Commitment.
Flexibility.
Attitude to Training.

References

1. G. Johnson and K. Scholes: "Exploring Corporate Strategy"; Prentice Hall International, 1984, p. 28.

2. R. Ashley Rawlins TD DL: "The Millennium Manager"; AuthorHouse, 2006. p. 17.

3. G. Johnson and K. Scholes: See Reference 1; p.336.

4. Edgar H. Schein: "The Role of the Founder in Creating Organisational Culture"; Organisational Dynamics, 1983.

5. G. Johnson and K. Scholes: See Reference 1; p. 299. H. Mintzberg: "The Structure of Organisations; Prentice Hall; 1979, pp. 285-287.

6. Mathew Arnold: "The Portable Mathew Arnold"; 1949, New York, The Viking Press; pp. 442-443.

7. R. H. Tawney: "Equality"; 1964, George Allen & Unwin Ltd. 3rd Impression 1975; pp. 35-36.

8. R. H. Tawney: "Equality"; See reference 7. p. 229.

PART THREE

Research Methodology

There are numerous ways of collecting research data, for example; questionnaire, interviews, observation etc.

Observation

There is a vast area of information for which observation is the only method available or suitable. Obviously; the study of records, mechanical processes, and animals fall into this category. Most small children cannot be questioned very successfully. Even amongst studies of human group processes, it is extremely difficult to gather useful information by questioning respondents - including the use of postal questionnaires -. People's interactions and involvement in group processes are usually such that, they are unable to report what happened accurately. Because of their commitment and loyalty to the group; they may report only the good things, they may report what is expected to happen and not what actually happened. This will corrupt the data collected and introduce bias into the results and analysis.

Another value of observation research methods result in the fact that, we can collect the original data ourselves at the time it occurs. We need not depend upon reports produced by others at a later date. Every respondent during questioning or reporting, filters the information he/she gives, no matter how well intentioned he/she is. Forgetting also occurs during questioning or reporting, and at times, there are reasons why the respondent may not want to report fully and clearly. Observation overcomes many of these deficiencies of questioning.

Observation research method can be successful in securing information, which most participants would ignore, either; because that information is so common and expected or because the participants do not see it as important or relevant. For example; if we are observing the sales activity in a department of a large store, there may be a mass of conditions that are of great interest to our research but which the normal shopper would consider to be unimportant. We can expect to learn only a part of the answers when questioning some respondents on matters such as:

- The condition of the weather.

- The day of the week.

- The time of the day.

- The number of employees in a department at the time of shopping.

- Customer traffic in the department at the time.

- The existence of special promotions in the department.

- Promotional activities in competing stores.

Observation is the only research method that can be used to successfully capture the whole event as it occurs. We may be interested in all the conditions surrounding a confrontation, at a bargaining session, between union and management representatives. These sessions may extend over a period of time, and any effort to study the unfolding of the negotiation process is greatly facilitated by the use of observation research method. Questioning could seldom provide the insight that would be provided by observation, for many of the aspects of the negotiation process.

Subjects usually seem to accept an observation type of intrusion better than questioning. Observation is less demanding of them and normally has less biasing effect on their conduct than does questioning. In addition, it is also possible to conduct disguised and unobtrusive observation studies, much more easily, than disguised questioning. For example; an observer could become a member of the group being observed, such disguise is not possible with questioning.

Limitations of Observation

There are also some research limitations of the observational method. A major problem or limitation is that, the observer must be at the scene of the event when it is taking place. Yet it is often impossible to predict where and when the event will occur. One way to guard against missing an event is to observe for prolonged periods until the event does occur, but this highlights another problem or disadvantage. That is to say, that observation is a slow and expensive process, which requires either human observers or some type of surveillance equipment, which is often costly.

Another limitation of observation research method is that, its most reliable results are restricted to data, which can be determined by overt action or surface indicators. To go below the surface, the observers must make inferences from surface indicators. Two observers will probably agree on the nature of various surface events, but the inferences they draw from such data are much more varied.

R. Ashley Rawlins TD. DL.

The use of observation is limited as a way of learning about the past. It is limited in a similar manner as a method by, which way of learning what is going on at present at some distant place. It is also difficult to gather information on such topics as; intentions, attitudes, opinions, or preferences. Any consideration of the merits of observation method, indicates that, it is a valuable research tool when used with care and understanding.

Some people restrict the concept of observation to "watching", but this is too narrow a view. It also involves listening and reading. Behavioural scientists tend to define observation in terms of animal or human behaviour, but this is also too narrow. In research, observation includes the full range of monitoring behavioural and non-behavioural activities and conditions which can roughly be classified into the following:

1.   Non-behavioural observation – reading analysis, physical condition analysis, physical process analysis.

2.   Behavioural observation – nonverbal analysis, linguistic analysis, spatial analysis.

Interview Research Method

Interviewing is a two-way purposeful conversation initiated by an interviewer, to obtain information that is relevant to the research purpose. The difference in roles between the interviewer and the respondent is pronounced. These participants are typically strangers; the interviewer dictates the topics and pattern of discussions. The consequences of the event are normally having minimal affect on the respondent. He/she is usually asked to provide information in the form of; facts, attitudes, opinions, and intentions, with little hope of receiving any immediate or direct benefit from his/her co-operation. However, if the interview is carried out successfully, it is a good data collection technique. Successful interview has the characteristic that a relationship of confidence and understanding exists between respondent and interviewer.

Interview situations are often new to the respondents and help is needed in defining his/her role. The interviewer can help by conveying the fact that the interview is confidential and important and that the interviewer is; friendly, ready to listen, and that the respondent can discuss the topics with; freedom from censure, coercion, or pressure. Under such conditions the respondent can obtain satisfaction in "opening up" without pressure being exerted.

One of the most difficult tasks in interviewing is to make certain that the answers adequately satisfy the question objectives. To do this, the interviewer must learn the objectives of each question from a study of the research objectives.

Advantages of Interview Method

There are some advantages as well as limitations to personal interviewing. The value of this research method is, the depth and detail of the information that can be secured. It exceeds in volume and quality, the information that can be secured from, say, telephone and mail. The interviewer can also do more things to improve the quality of the information received than with other research methods. The interviewer can; note the conditions of the interview, probe with additional questions when appropriate, and request to see a product that the respondent claims to have, and gather other supplemental information through observation.

The interviewer also has more control over the personal interview than with other research methods. He/she can pre-screen to ensure that the correct respondent is replying. The interviewer can influence and control interviewing conditions. He/she can use special scoring devices, visual materials etc. The interviewer can make adjustments to the language of the interview because the problems and effects that the interview is having on the respondent can be observed.

Disadvantages of Interview Method

The major problem with observation research method is that it is costly, both in money and time. Costs are particularly high, more so in places where the research covers a large geographic area. Another problem is that interviewers who alter the questions being asked may affect the results. The attitude of the interviewer and the way the questions are asked may introduce bias into the respondents' replies.

An interviewer can distort the results of any research by; inappropriate suggestions, word emphasis, tone of voice, and question rephrasing. Such activities may be premeditated or merely due to carelessness. These problems must be taken into account when analysing the results of the research.

Telephone Interviewing

Because of the widespread acceptance of the telephone, as a necessary communication device, telephone interviewing has some advantages over some alternative methods; however, there are also some disadvantages.

One advantage of telephone interviewing is its low cost. Travel time can be reduced because all calls can be made from a single location. Telephone interviewing is especially economical when there are many call-backs to make and respondents are widely scattered.

With telephone interviewing, interview bias is normally reduced because of the lack of face-to-face contact between interviewer and respondent. A study can be planned and carried out in a few days over a wide geographical area.

There are also limitations to the use of telephones for research. There are large numbers of obsolete numbers and newly located buildings and households for which numbers have not yet been issued/published. Limits on the length of interviews are another disadvantage of telephone interviewing, but the degree of the limitation depends on the type of respondent and his/her interest in the topic being researched.

With telephone interviewing, it is not possible to use; budgets, maps, illustrations, or complex scales. Complexity of the questioning and the use of sorting techniques are also limited.

Choice of Research Methods

The choice of one particular research method in preference to another should not be based on an arbitrary decision, because some methods of data collection will be more appropriate than others, in any given situation. However, in the real world, the researcher quite often has to compromise between what he/she wants to do and what he/she can do.

My research for this book was no different. I wanted to canvas the opinions of all employees and strategic managers of Leeds design Consultancy, who were in post when the TQM programme was introduced. The objective of my research was twofold:

1.   To establish whether the programme was achieving its original objectives of; greater employee involvement in decision-making, change in employee's attitude to work and towards each other, change in organisational culture.

2.   To ascertain how individual members viewed and judged the success of the TQM programme.

At this stage the Leeds Design Consultancy TQM programme involved 160 people. Whatever method of research I adopted, if it was to reach 160 people spread throughout the City Council, it would be very time-consuming. Because of; the flexible working patterns of employees of Leeds City Council, my own work load and the fact that, at that stage, I was no longer employed by Leeds City Council but by Nottingham City Council, it was not practical to attempt to interview the whole of that organisation.

As the objective of my research was to discover; how present and past employees of Leeds Design Consultancy judged the success of the TQM programme, I decided to conduct a series of in-depth interviews with managers and other staff representing all of the disciplines covered by the Leeds Design Consultancy. Armed with the results of those interviews and the organisational background, I could ascertain the opinion of the people who were involved with; the planning, implementation and the effects of the TQM programme. I also interviewed people from other local authority organisations, and studied reports of other organisations where TQM programmes have been introduced.

I had prepared a number of questions, but the idea was, to get the respondents to do most of the talking and to use the questions as prompts, only, if the information received fell short of my expectations.

In-Depth Interviewing

In-depth interviewing is probably the most popular method of; cultural, attitudinal and motivational method of research, and although the number of my interviewees were limited to just 20 to 30 people, the time for each interview was in excess of 120 minutes, and could be classed as in-depth interviews. In-depth interviewing was a very time consuming way of gathering my research information. Although the number of people interviewed fell far short of the number that I would have preferred and also short of what is considered as ideal, it was something that, under the circumstances, I felt that I could cope with.

However, there are several drawbacks in tackling my research in this way. For example, such a small sample could hardly be regarded as representative. Mostyn [1] suggests that typically a motivational study utilising in-depth interviewing would consist of between 50 and 100 interviews, with 60 being optimal. Obviously the number of interviews I would conduct was less than that suggested by Mostyn. However, other pieces of significant research have been based on far less than 60 interviews, for example, the J. W. T. document [2].

Another problem in adopting this approach was, interview contamination. This is always a problem for the interviewer, and in some cases this was exaggerated by the fact that the respondent as a member of management may have identified me and so modified their answers. One could reasonably expect some interviewees to be constrained by this fact, but as I could not eliminate this influence I just had to minimise its effect by emphasising that my research was independent of any studies being carried out by others, for the Leeds Design Consultancy or the City Council, and that their statements would be treated as confidential information where necessary.

Apart from the above reservations, there are a number of generally accepted advantages and disadvantages associated with interviewing, in-depth or otherwise. Briefly stated, these are:

Advantages

- Probing – the interviewer has the opportunity to get beyond the superficial answer, by asking probing questions followed by qualifying questions.

- Recall – probing questions allow the interviewee to recall past attitudes and opinions through their recollection, to the interviewer.

- Rapport – as the interview progresses, interviewer and interviewee share a common experience, which if properly handled, should help the interviewer understand the interviewee, and should leave the interviewee feeling that he/she was understood.

Disadvantages

- Interviewer skill – interviewing does require skilful handling, but with training and experience some of the pitfalls associated with interviewing, such as; mirror image, halo effect etc, can be recognised by the interviewer and their effects neutralised.

- Barriers – can be created between interviewer and interviewee that could prevent the objectives of the interview being achieved.

- General problems – interviewing is very time-consuming, and more so when collecting large quantities of data. The results of interviews are difficult to analyse statistically, and unstructured questioning techniques may result in each interview pursuing different objectives or going down different paths.

In spite of all the problems, difficulties and disadvantages of interview research methods highlighted above, including the limitations placed on my study associated with the number of interviews, I felt that interviewing was still the best method of gathering my information and data in preparation for this book.

Interviewing Format

Depth interviewing according to Newman [3]:

> "… refers to the psychological level of material; an in-depth to the extent that it uncovers basic predispositions, unconscious feelings, needs, conflicts, fears, etc."

Mostyn [4] argues that in theory, depth interviews do not include questions; instead, the interviewee is encouraged to talk himself out as long as certain key areas are covered. I agree with the argument put forward by Mostyn, however, covering key areas is an important point as far as the objectives of my research was concerned. So I decided to conduct the interviews with the use of questions, so that I could prompt the interviewees and as far as possible, eliminate both inconsistency and prolonged periods of silence, if the interviewees were not particularly forthcoming. Never the less, if the key areas were being covered without the use of the questions, I did not use the questions but just allow the interviewees to talk without interruptions. I did not put any constraint on the interviewees, except time limits, but I took notes of everything that was said, and at a later date, put the various statements together in a coherent way to make sense for the reader.

Obviously, any questions had to de carefully constructed. For example, closed questions such as; "do you like . . .?" are likely to get a "yes" or "no" response and nothing else. Open questions allow the interviewee to think and express an opinion. Questions directed at key areas set the tone and direction of the interview. However, the initial question will need to be followed up by a qualifying question, if the interviewer feels that the response does not adequately cover the area of his research. The qualifying questions may vary from interview to interview, depending on the response to the initial question. Nevertheless, qualifying questions are necessary to clarify the responses.

Interview Results

Interpreting the results of the interviews is not easy. There are a number of problems associated with this task.

In the interview, the interviewer cannot hope to record every word verbatim, unless a tape recorder is used. "Pet words" can creep into the recorded answers, misleading the interpreter. One can only be aware that this problem exists and try to avoid it.

Another problem that can occur during the interview is the inability of the interviewee to understand the question and be articulate enough to reply adequately.

Mostyn [5] argues that the interpretation of interviews requires a thorough knowledge of human behaviour. However, Newman [6] gives an example of a study based on interviews in which a variety of types of social scientists participated without comparable results. The outcome of this work suggests that to successfully interpret in-depth interviews is more likely to depend on knowledge of the theories, combined with inductive reasoning pattern, rather than deductive reasoning.

In the interpretation of the results of my interviews, I found it necessary to use both inductive and deductive reasoning patterns.

Interpretation Method

There are at least four methods of interpreting the results of studies using in-depth interviews. These are:

1. Illustrative insight

2. Frequency statements

3. Statements of co-variance

4. Statements of casual relationship

All of these methods are appropriate to my study using in-depth interviews. For example; frequency statements and statements of co-variance rely on a reasonable response to a question. My study, which involved about 20 to 30 interviews, could only give an illustrative insight into my chosen area for this study, but I felt that this number was adequate for my study.

Statisticians suggest that descriptive data is particularly influential with policy-makers because its concrete reality has a more persuasive impact than purely statistical information.

The value of adopting this approach lies in its fruitfulness and its potential utility. A good idea does not need to be representative in a statistical sense. Illustrative insight is characteristic of interviews and open ended questioning techniques. Very little in the way of analysis is needed. Statements or anecdote may have to be depersonalised in order to respect the respondents' confidentiality.

During my research for this book using in-depth interviews, I was requested to observe or respect such respondents' confidentiality. For example; one Senior Architect said:

> "You could print anything you like, from the interview, provided you do not print my name."

I promised all respondents that their confidentiality would be respected.

Questionnaire

I stated earlier that using questionnaires was not a useful method of gathering information when studying human group processes, because involvement in-group processes is usually such that they are unable to report accurately what happened. Because of their loyalty to the group, they may report only the good things. They may report what is expected to happen and not what actually happened. They may also compare answers. This will introduce bias into the study. However, because I wanted to reach as many individuals as possible and interviewing everyone was out of the question, I decided to supplement the in-depth interviews by circulating all members, in whom I was interested, with questionnaires.

I sent the questionnaires to 200 individuals and 160 were returned. This is a very high rate considering that I was no longer one of their colleague and some individuals had moved on to other things and other organisations. The questionnaire is outlined below.

The Questions – When answering the questions, put an "X" in the appropriate box.

QUESTIONS	YES	NO	DON'T KNOW
Does your organisation have set objectives?			
Does your organisation have a mission statement?			
Was reorganisation necessary?			
Did reorganisation occur too quickly?			
Are you committed to your organisation objectives?			
Does Annual Appraisal motivate you?			
Does Performance Related Pay motivate you?			

Does your organisation set standards for performance?			
Is your work checked or inspected?			
Do you get satisfaction from doing your present job?			
Were you affected by the recent reorganisation?			
Have your working practices changed since reorganisation?			
Is career development possible in your present Job?			
Do you have access to staff training?			
Are the necessary training associated with your work available?			
Are your future prospects with the organisation good?			
Do you receive information by Memos?			
Do you receive information by newsletter?			
Do you receive information by team briefing?			
Do you report to more than one person?			
Is satisfying clients/customers your first priority?			
Do you have more than 12 team briefings in a year?			
Do you have more than one skills review in a year?			

Were you involved in consultations before reorganisation?			
Do you think that agreed requirements with customers are important?			
Do political issues affect the quality of your work?			
Do financial issues affect the quality of your work?			
Do legal issues affect the quality of your work?			
Do the requirements of professional institution affect the quality of your work?			
Do you use benchmarking in your quality checks?			
Can you recognise more than 30% of people in your organisation?			

In your view, which of the following statements best describe a "quality service"? You may select up to four statements. Mark your selection with an "X" in the box.

Quality is what the customer says it is.	
Quality is what the officer and professional say it is.	
Quality is customer satisfaction.	
Quality is responding quickly to customers' complaints.	
Quality is the cheapest job.	

Quality is doing a full day's work for a full day's pay.	
Quality is having a good inspection team to check and reject faulty work.	
Quality is getting it right first time, every time.	
Quality is correcting other people's mistakes before providing the service.	
Quality is good teamwork.	
Quality is "Just in Time".	

In your view, which of the following statements best describe "Total Quality"? You may select any number of statements. Mark your selection with an "X" in the box.

Strive to prevent problems.	
Meeting customer/supplier requirements.	
Getting things right first time, every time.	
Eliminating failures.	
Maximising the talents and creativity of all our people.	

References

1. B. Mostyn: "Handbook of Motivational and Attitude Research Techniques". MCB Publications, p. 22.

2. B. Mostyn: See Reference 1, p. 23. T. W. Thompson: "A Practicum of Marketing Research", 1961, Marketing Research Dept. (Published for Clients and Staff only), New York.

3. J. W. Newman: "Motivation Research and Marketing Management", 1957, Harvard University Press.

4. B. Mostyn: See Reference 1, p. 19.

5. B. Mostyn: See Reference 1, p. 26.

6. J. W. Newman: See Reference 3.

PART FOUR

THE IMPLICATIONS

Topic Areas

I have already stated that it was necessary to identify the key areas of the research. In trying to gain an insight into the areas I considered relevant to my study, I chose the following key areas to explore:

Understanding the TQM Concept

This area was interested for a number of reasons. Firstly, had the respondent a good understanding of the underlying concept? Secondly, did the respondents' understanding influence the expectations of the member and if it did, had these expectations been met?

Expectations

Exposure to the concept and participation in the TQM programme would highlight the potential benefits of TQM for both the organisation and the member of staff. Had the members of staff identified these benefits, and if they had, had these been used as a further measure of success?

Realisation

Had the expectations been met and to what degree?

Success or Failure

What criteria were members of staff and others using to judge the success or failure of the TQM programme? Did they perceive the programme as being a success or failure?

Involvement

Did those people who were involved with the TQM programme feel that their membership had given them a greater degree of involvement in the decisions that directly affected them?

Attitudes and Relationships

Had the attitudes of these members of staff, who were involved in the TQM programme, changed towards their; supervisors, work colleagues or the Job they did and if so, how?

Having decided which topic areas I wanted to explore, I was then in a position where I could direct the interviews in such a way that they would address the topic areas, but not necessarily in the sequence listed above. The idea adopted was to; allow the respondent to talk freely and not to disturb the natural flow of the discussion unless it depart wide of the topic areas.

I now had the basis for my interviews, but still had to decide where the interviews would be conducted, and how long each interview would take.

The interview location was important, but in practice I left the choice of location to the interviewees. The choice of location was varied; some choose their works conference room, some their work area, some their homes, and others my home. There was no shortage of time, even where the interviews took place in the work area, and in all cases the atmosphere was relaxed.

It was my intention to treat the respondents to refreshments during the interviews, but in the cases where the respondents choose to be interviewed in their homes or at their place of work, I was treated to refreshments.

I was then faced with the problem of note taking. How can I keep the discussion flowing naturally and take notes at the same time? I decided to use an electronic recorder. Fortunately, all respondents accepted this idea. The following were examples of some of the statements made by respondents:

Several of the respondents' response to this idea was that it is a good idea. One respondent stated: "I do not have to wait for you to take notes, I can talk naturally."

Having first discussed, by telephone; the reason, objective and aims of the interview with the respondents, one respondent got into his stride before I switched on the recorder and he said:

> "Your recorder was not switched on so I will
> start again".

After one of the interviews that took place at my house, I was walking the respondent to his car when he made a statement. I was hoping that I would remember that statement later, when he said:

> "If you want record that, switch your machine
> on and I will repeat that statement."

I felt that the use of the recorder was very well received, but it is time consuming and could be very expensive. However, I kept the expense to a minimum by using the same tapes for all of the interviews. This process created additional pressure for me because it meant that after each interview, I had to play the recorded interview and make notes before going on to the next interview. That was also very time consuming. A one and a half hour interview took a further two hours in note taking, so each interview took a total time of over three and a half hours.

Target Population

I felt that in selecting my target population and do justice to the subject, it was necessary for me to identify TQM members who would not object to being interviewed. This way I would save a lot of time by not having too many wasted journeys although not looking for members who were all positive about TQM programmes. To this end I used my personal Knowledge of individual members, used the telephone to discuss with potential respondents, my reason for choosing them, the aims and objectives of the interviews and request their assistance in this way. A number of employees of Nottingham City Council, who were employed in departments where the TQM programmes have been implemented were also targeted. Members to be interviewed were chosen based on the following criteria:

- The number and size of projects completed.

- Members working relationships with senior managers.

- Length of time spent in the TQM programme.

- Accessibility.

- Continuous employment within the TQM programme.

I had some knowledge of members from Leeds City Council who were involved with the TQM programme that was introduced into one of its departments. This knowledge was gained during my employment with Leeds Design Consultancy. Although I had a good knowledge of about 70% of the people from Nottingham City Council, who were involved in that organisation's TQM programme, because I was also involved with the implementation of that programme, I had very little knowledge of members from Nottingham City Council's Department of Public Works. I also had no knowledge of any individual members who were involved in the Barnsley City Council Architects Department's TQM programme. Nottingham City Council purchased a copy of the Barnsley TQM report so I was able to study that and felt that interviewing members of staff from that organisation were not necessary.

Interviewees Background

During my research for this book I interviewed twenty past and present employees of the Leeds Design Consultancy and ten members from several departments of Nottingham City Council. The people interviewed have served at varying levels of seniority in their organisations.

The following are the background of those who were interviewed from Leeds City Council's Design Consultancy:

The previous Head of Building Services Engineering who; took early retirement on health grounds in 1995 and witnessed all the changes and reorganisations since 1974 and was part of the senior management team.

The previous Deputy Head of Building Services Engineering and Head of Mechanical Services who; took early retirement because of poor health in 1994 and witnessed all the changes and reorganisations since 1974. He was part of the senior management team.

Two Senior Design Engineers who; were team leaders, witnessed most of the changes and reorganisations since 1974 and are junior managers.

Three Engineers who; witnessed all of the changes and reorganisations since 1974 mainly as Technicians, were promoted to Assistant Engineers in 1986 and Engineers in 1989.

Two Engineers who; joined Leeds Design Consultancy in 1989 as Assistant Engineers after working in private industry.

Two Assistant Engineers who, joined Leeds Design Consultancy in 1989 on promotion from another local authority organisation.

The City Architect who; was appointed in 1987, was a major player in the last reorganisation and responsible for setting up and implementing the TQM programme.

Two Architects who; witnessed all of the changes and reorganisations since 1974 and took early retirement in November 1993 but continued to work for the Leeds Design Consultancy as self employed consultants. They worked from offices, set up in his home.

Three Senior Architects who, have been in local government since 1970. They worked in the Architect's Department of the West Riding County Council and moved to Leeds City Council in 1974 when the West Riding was disbanded under Unitary Status.

A Chief Architect who; was a Senior Architect with the West Riding County Council before Unitary Status, moved to Leeds City Council After Unitary Status in 1974 as an Architect but was on protected salary until the last reorganisation when he was appointed Senior Architect and later was promoted to the position of Chief Architect, after the previous Chief Architect was forced to retire, due to ill health.

A Chief Structural Engineer who; witnessed all the changes and reorganisations since 1974 and as a senior manager, was part of the management team during the last reorganisation. He was also involved with the introduction of the TQM programme into the organisation.

The following are the background of those who were interviewed from Nottingham City Council:

The Quality Manager of Nottingham City Council's Public Works Department who; was responsible for the development and implementation of Quality Systems into that department in 1990 and was responsible for the maintenance of those systems after implementation. He was part of part of Nottingham City Council's TQM development team and was responsible for driving the implementation of the TQM programme throughout the Public Works Department. The Public Works Department was awarded the "Quality Mark" in 1992.

The Assistant Quality Manager of Nottingham City Council's Public Works Department.

The Head of Building Services Engineering of Nottingham City Council who; was involved in the TQM programme from the initial stages and was responsible for driving the implementation of the TQM programme throughout Nottingham City Council's Building Services Engineering Department.

The Chief Architect of Nottingham City Council who; joined Nottingham City Council after the decision was taken, that the organisation will development and implement a TQM programme. She was part of the TQM development team and was also responsible for driving the implementation of the TQM programme throughout the Architects Department and Administration Team.

A Senior Architect who, joined Nottingham City Council on promotion in 1989 after several years with Nottingham County Council.

A Chief Building Surveyor who, was a Senior Architect with Nottingham County Council and joined Nottingham City Council on promotion in 1990.

Two Senior Design Engineers and Team Leaders who, joined Nottingham City Council in 1980 after several years with a private contracting organisations.

A member of the Strategic Management Development Team who, joined Nottingham City Council in 1990 after a number of years working for a firm of Management Consultants.

A member of the Strategic Management Development Team who, joined Nottingham City Council in 1980 after graduating from university. He has worked in the Chief Executive's office since joining the organisation.

The works carried out by the above interviewees are as follows:

- The Strategic Management Development Team is a group of Senior Managers working under the leadership of the Chief Executive Officer to; develop, drive and monitor the TQM programme for Nottingham City Council. It is also responsible for arrangement of; courses, seminars and conferences associated with the TQM programme and Managing Change initiatives for managers employed by Nottingham City Council.

- Architectural and Clerk of Works services – Design for the implementation of the City Councils' Capital Building Programme. Advice to other City Councils' departments on all architectural matters. Service to the Leeds City Council's Airport Joint Committee. Advice on the appointment and supervision of private consultants associated with the Capital Programme projects. Professional direction of the tendering procedure.

- Mechanical and Electrical Engineering – Develop, design and monitor all Building Engineering Services associated with the capital programme for all other City Council's Departments. Maintenance of building services in all City Council's buildings. Engineering advisory service to all City Council's departments.

- Energy Management – Advice all departments on energy conservation issue. Negotiate energy and water charges with the respective providers on behalf of all City Council's departments.

- Surveyors - Surveys of buildings to establish condition and need for maintenance, repair, alterations and improvements. Preparation of drawings, specifications and tender documents for works required.

- Structural Engineers - Provision of structural engineering services, from inception to completion, associated with the implementation of the City Councils' capital programme. Advice to the City Council and the Airport Joint Committee on the appointment of contractors and consultants.

- Administration - The provision of support services to the City Councils' Director of Planning.

The Analysis

In trying to make sense of the information I had gathered from the interviews, I set out to identify key words in the respondents' answers, which I thought were relevant to the study, for example; customer requirements, customer satisfaction, quality, responsibility, motivation, training, communication, commitment, right first time, relationship between staff, relationship between staff and managers, career development etc. I then categorised the responses to establish some commonality between the responses of the different respondents.

Understanding the Concept

Overall, there seems to be a good understanding amongst the respondents of the TQM concept. The definitions given by respondents, ranged from almost textbook definition by senior members - Senior Architects, Engineers and above - who had had formal management training, to very simple but valid definitions from other members of staff who had received no management training. This indicates that members of staff at management levels have received some formal management training, however, those members of staff who were also members of professional organisations or institutions seems to have a better understanding of the TQM concept and of its relevance to their organisation's efficiency.

Expectations

What individual members of staff expected to gain from the TQM programme varied considerably. It was rather interesting to learn that almost all of the senior members of staff, who were interviewed, highlighted the potential of the TQM programme to change staff attitudes in a positive way and that that would benefit the organisation, its customers and enhance its service provision. However, a very high proportion of those interviewed and were employed by Leeds City Council, seemed to hold negative attitudes towards senior management in general and towards the organisation as a whole. This was due mainly to a lack of trust.

One senior manager from Leeds City Council said:

> "The TQM programme was successful in broad terms. It achieved its objectives to the extent it was; more streamlined, more

> efficient, people are more committed to the organisation, people are working as a team rather than competing with each other to gain recognition, management's tasks are much easier and we can now compete with private organisations and win. Some people may have been hurt by the process and it might have caused some people to do things which they might not otherwise have done. For example; some people took early retirement, some people were transferred to other City Council departments after applying for positions with those departments, some left the City Council altogether and joined private organisations, whilst others retrained for other careers such as teaching and lecturing. Some of those who took early retirement came off reasonably well out of the process. It is fair to say that the process was substantially successful. The TQM programme achieved its objectives."

All of the senior managers who were interviewed, including the City Architect, made similar statements.

I met one former employee who underwent retraining and became a teacher and he said:

> "It was the best thing that could have happened to me because I am doing very well as a teacher and I am enjoying it."

One Engineer who is employed by Leeds City Council said:

> "After the introduction of The TQM programme, three engineers left the department, they were never replaced but the work load remained the same. I made an application to be regraded. I do not trust the Head of Building Engineering Services so I made my application in writing to the City Architect and my regrade was granted. There is so much pressure; you just do not get time to yourself. One of my colleagues had a nervous breakdown and I am sure that it is because of the pressure of work."

I was rather surprised to hear this engineer states that one of his colleagues had a nervous breakdown and that it was due to the pressure of work. That may well be the case, I cannot argue in favour of or against this engineer's points of view or his assumptions. What I can say, however, is that the person in question was a Mechanical Engineer, recruited by Leeds City Council, during my employment with the City Council, as a manager in that department. He previously worked in private industry, suffered a similar nervous breakdown and after his recovery, was employed by Leeds City Council under its equal opportunities policy. The above Engineer who made the assumption that his colleague's illness was due to his work with Leeds City Council would not have knowledge of the above information because he was recruited by Leeds City Council, from another Local Authority, about three years after his colleague and was a junior engineer at that time.

Other Engineers below the management grades/levels made similar statements. It seems, therefore, that expectations differ widely between management and non-management grades. However, all grades agreed that pay and conditions have improved. Whilst all engineers agreed that pay and conditions have improved, Nottingham City Council's Engineers argued that this was not due to the TQM programme since pay and conditions have improved in all Local Authority Organisations throughout the United Kingdom. This argument was due to the fact that Leeds City Council used the Staff Appraisal System - part of the TQM programme - as a financial reward system for staff who were involved in the TQM programme, where as Nottingham City Council used the Staff Appraisal System as part of the staff development linked to the TQM programme. This was made easy for Nottingham City Council because the organisation as a whole was involved in the TQM programme with the Chief Executive driving it.

Commitment to the Organisation's Objectives

City Council's employees provide the manpower resources and they are also stakeholders – members of the public/ community who pay for the services through their income taxes, council taxes and other community charges – they therefore, have a vested interest in the successful achievement of the organisation's corporate objectives.

The City Architect told one Architect that he could not have Voluntary Early Retirement, to which the Architect replied, "I will come to work and do nothing". The City Architect replied; "you will never do that, because you are a professional". The City Architect, in this case is suggesting that as a professional person, the Architect is expected to operate to a code of practise set by the professional institution to which all qualified Architects are expected to be members and is one of the conditions of their employment - this was a personal experience -. Most of the people interviewed said that they were highly committed to the organisation's objectives.

During the interview with the City Architect, he said that he identified people whom he thought would not fit into the new culture of; continuous change, commitment to organisation's objectives, teamwork and value for money. Those employees, who were identified, were; redeployed, transferred to other departments or given early retirement. The City Architect agreed that those people whom it was felt will not give total commitment to their profession, were those who were transferred to other City Council departments or redeployed. However, he disagreed with me when I suggested to him that those employees whom he identified as lacking in commitment were mainly those who objected to the move from Sweet Street to Merrion House.

One Engineer who is employed by Leeds City Council said:

> "I am on leave now but I have to do work at home to meet some silly target which was set by the Chief Engineer, without agreement or consultation with me. I have to work a lot of extra hours - Evenings, Saturdays, and Sundays - because the customers or clients have been promised the design completion by a certain date. I get a lot of side tracking during the day; sorting out problems associated with other jobs, chasing information from other departments but I am committed to satisfying the customer. If the customer is happy, then I am happy. After all, the customer pays the money so he has the right to call the tune."

A very high proportion of those people interviewed, who were employed by Leeds City Council, seems to be happy with the Staff Appraisal System mainly because it linked performance with additional payment but if the time spent working on projects at home were taken into account, they would realise that the additional payment gained through Performance Related Pay (PRP) do not adequately compensate for that extra time, the loss of leisure or rest periods. However, private organisations operate in this way and if local authority employees are expected to compete with private organisations, then they will have to adopt the same attitude to work and meeting completion dates and targets.

Another Engineer Said:

> "I have been employed by Leeds City Council for 17 years but, I have never worked as hard as I have done over the last 36 months. I go home feeling that I have done a good days work. Occasionally, if I have a push on, to get a job completed, I will work late into the evening or take the work home with me. I am even taking specifications with me and writing them at home, however, I cannot take drawings and do them at home because I do not have the space, proper equipments and adequate lighting. I work on specifications on Saturdays, Sundays and on evenings to get stuff out, to meet impossible targets."

One Architect who is employed by Leeds City Council Said:

"I had to carry over, 18 days annual leave last year. I just did not have the time to take those annual leave days and there are several of my colleagues in a similar position. We can now work overtime and get either payment or a mixture of payment plus time off. The department has become very flexible in its approach to work, so people move about and help each other out. I think Don Taylor - the City Architect - did the right thing. I do not think you can change people so easily. Trying to change an organisation's culture by training people, does not always work. To do the job properly, you have to be interested in it for a start that is the prime motivator. You have to be interested in your job and I do not see how you can make people interested in something that they are not interested in. Yes, I am sure he did it the right way".

All Engineers and Architects made similar statements but it seems that only the Building Services Engineers have imposed time scales and targets. The Engineers who were not at managerial levels could not understand the logic in an organisation where staff at similar levels within the organisation was treated differently. I could not understand it either. I could not understand the fact that Architects were paid overtime for extra time worked and had more flexibility than Engineers. However, it seems to me that the reason for the Architects having less pressure of work than the Engineers has more to do with team work than flexibility or target setting. There also seems to be different styles of management within the department and this has caused some employees to have no trust in their managers. I feel that the City Architect needs to put more effort into management training so that all employees are managed equally. The City Architect agreed with me on this point. All the respondents seem to be committed to the organisation's objectives.

Appraisal and Performance Related Pay

A Senior Architect who is employed by Leeds City Council said:

> "Performance Related Pay (PRP) is working well. It is an advantage because it tends to keep people on their toes, if they know they are going to be interviewed. You see, previously, you just get a pay award regardless of whether you had worked for it or not. Now you have to earn it so that keeps you on the ball."

The same Architect went on to say:

> "They have a pot of money which they know they have to distribute around the office, so in a way, the total sum of money available for distribution is all predetermined because, there is a limit to the amount they can have in terms of extra payment for people for the coming year. So if every body were perfect examples of what they should be and got top marks, the system just would not work. There has to be an even distribution of payouts."

One Leeds City Council Engineer Said:

"I get the same comments every year. I have worked harder this year than I did last year and I expected my PRP to reflect that, but it remains the same. I think they should scrap PRP and share out the additional cash evenly amongst all staff and give it at Christmas time as a Christmas box."

Everyone should be treated; equally, fairly, with dignity and respect at work and it is in every manager's interest to promote a fair environment in which people can work. Unequal and unfair treatment are not only unacceptable on morale grounds but may, if not checked or is handled badly give rise to a claim of discrimination on the grounds of; sex, race, disability, sexual orientation, religion, belief or age.

This can create serious problems for an organisation including:

- Poor morale and poor employee relations.

- Loss of respect and trust for managers.

- Poor performance and reduced productivity.

- High rate of absence.

- Damage to the organisation's reputation.

The appraisal system, part of the TQM programme, was set up to reward people for achievement. The appraisal system was introduced to appraise staff effectiveness by monitoring their performance over a 12-month period. Pay increases over and above those negotiated by the trade union are based on individual staff achievement as detailed in his/

her last signed annual appraisal. Some people are against this system because they say that senior managers may introduce bias into the system but since this is expected to be an open system of appraisal where the appraisement is discussed with the individual being appraised, this problem of bias should not arise. However, there seems to be some problems of inequalities within the organisation, resulting in staff being treated differently. We have details of some employees arguing that PRP is the best way of getting people to improve their performance and operate more efficiently and effectively with corresponding acknowledgement and rewards, whilst other employees in the same department argue that PRP is not working because year after year their; extra effort, improved efficiency and effectiveness are not acknowledged or rewarded. However, from what some of the respondents have told me, it is clear that the problems causing inequalities and perceived differences is due to more than the difference in management styles. It seems to me that in the cases where employees are happy and are being acknowledged and rewarded for improved efficiency, those employees are working as a team and they are all benefiting from that teamwork approach. On the other hand, in the cases where employees are; unhappy, frustrated and feel that their hard work and improved performance are not being acknowledged are rewarded, those employees seems not to be working as a team but in competition with each other, which makes their combined efforts less effective, hence less efficient.

Senior Managers argue that annual appraisal is the best way to motivate staff but, some members of staff argue that, what ever their performance, they receive the same comments and percentage points each year, so they are not motivated by annual appraisal. This situation presents a dilemma for senior managers and they will have to put more effort into communicating to other members of staff that the system is unbiased and that an appraisal system is one of the ways of monitoring staff performance and customer satisfaction in the Service or Public Sector. However, I feel that annual appraisals should be linked to staff development and not to pay.

Organisations should establish a written "staff appraisal policy" that includes the following:

- State what results the appraisal interviews are intended to achieve, and how these will be measured.

- Show how the organisation's appraisal system, for monitoring employees' performance, is linked to; the organisation's improvement, self-evaluation and development planning.

- Show how the organisation will seek to achieve consistency of treatment and fairness between those employees with similar experiences or levels of responsibility.

- Set out the timing of the cycle; this should include a departmental observation protocol.

- Provide appraisal system training for all employees, this being made available as the need arises.

- State the arrangements for monitoring and evaluating the staff appraisal policy.

Structured Questioning

Managers should use the staff appraisal system and "structured questioning", during the appraisal interview, in a way that allow both the manager and the staff being appraised. The following is an example of "structured questioning":

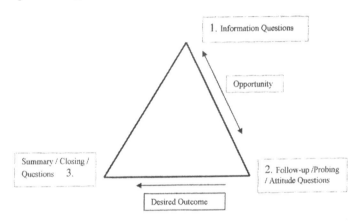

Starting Points:

- Why am I asking this question?

- What outcome am I looking for?

Level 1. Information Questions - the event for example; problem or opportunity -:

- Tell me about _____

- Explain _____

- Describe _____

Level 2. Follow-up / Probing Questions - attitudes for example; concerns, consequences, wants -:

- Who will benefit from this idea?

- What objectives did we set last time?

- When do we want to try it out?

- Where did you learn that new idea?

- Why is that important to you?

- How do you plan to follow it through?

Level 3. Closing Questions - the outcome for example; test understanding, gain commitment, agree solution -:

- Are we agreed on that?

- Shall we go ahead with that?

- What would you do differently next time?

- How would you go about that?

- How would you build on that?

Job Satisfaction

To feel a sense of achievement, people require satisfaction from their present job. Without job satisfaction I feel that people will have no commitment to the organisation's objectives and will not give 100% effort, or any way near that, to their work. If this is the case, and I believe it is, then performance monitoring will be meaning-less, however, this is not the case in this organisation because all its employees who were interviewed said that they get satisfaction from their present job.

The organisation should look at other less divisive ways of rewarding good performance. High performing employees can be given the more interesting projects to work on, and more discretion over the way that they allocate their time to those projects. They can also be given more influence in the team or access to opportunities for advancement within the organisation. This exercise can be done in such a way, that employees are being rewarded with other things that they value and this does not have to involve paying them more.

TQM requires everyone in the organisation to work together as a team and from my experience; people will only work together as a team if they are satisfied with their job and are committed to quality improvement.

Training and Career Development

Some of the people interviewed, agreed that there is a lot of training taking place at this point in time, but says that those training courses had nothing to do with staff development or new techniques in their technical work. Most of the training, they argued, is to do with the Government's new legislations on; health and safety matters, Compulsory Competitive Tendering (CCT) etc. Such courses, they argued, do not help in career development and because of financial constraint; technical and managerial courses that will help career development are not available. However, those who are at the senior levels and who were promoted as a result of the organisation restructure, agreed that staff training was inadequate but that career development and job prospects are good.

All employees should be given access to development opportunities. This is one of the keys to staff motivation; however, it seems that this organisation is failing to provide adequate development initiatives. If this organisation is serious about reversing the current trend on staff retention, and senior managers say they are, then it will have to address this issue and develop other incentives, besides pay, that suit both employee and organisational needs. Organisations that adopt this principle are more likely to keep its staff motivated and enthusiastic about their jobs. This will result in improved services and more satisfied customers.

The organisation will need to take a holistic approach, to make sure that all employees understand and appreciate the worth of these less tangible, cashless rewards. If managers give employees something as a benefit, then you have to make sure that they know about it. Managers have to make sure that employees know what the value is to them. Managers in an organisation like this, where most of the employees are either professionals or are working towards professional status, have to try and get people to think more strategically about their work and the service they provide rather than thinking about the size of the pay cheque going into their banks at the end of the month.

If TQM is to be successful in this organisation or any other local authority organisations, then these organisations must focus on giving their customers - client groups and the public - best value for money. This is very important and it is a real challenge since the customers are unable to show dissatisfaction by taking their custom elsewhere. A number of other local authority organisations, have used pay and rewards to drive up performance, for example; some have used performance related pay schemes that rewards managers for creating a positive working climate within their teams. This idea came about in response to research that shows, statistical evidence, that the better the organisational climate, the more successful that organisation will be. In those organisations, managers are issued agreed performance contracts which list key job objectives for the following year and also set agreed targets for whatever improvements, in climate, may be deemed necessary. In organisations where I have been involved with this, managers were asked to; identify what climate change was required in their areas or teams to achieve improvements, set realistic targets to achieve those improvements and then meet with their line managers to validate and agreed those targets.

Communication

Most of the people interviewed, agreed that communication is good, however, they still blamed poor communication for any lack of commitment to the organisation's objectives. From my research, it seems to me that proper systems are in place to support good communication within the organisation, with the majority of employees having more than one staff reviews per month. Employees also receive other departmental information in the form of memos, newsletters and news updates.

Managing is about teamwork and leadership; that goes for all organisations not just local authorities or the public sector organisations. This means that there has to be team leaders who will stamp out poor or bad communication and, after taking advice from other members of the team and assessing all available information, will decide on the best action to be taken, thus ensuring that the whole team works together to achieve the best service for the organisation and its customers.

If we look at how organisations operate in today's climate, we will se that the organisational hierarchy is still very much alive but that it seems to have been modified slightly to allow members of the team to have more involvement than previously, in the decision-making process. This could work well to the benefit of the organisation and its customers, only if the team leader consults well with the team and is able to make decisions based on those consultations.

Issues Affecting the Quality of Service Provision

A recently retired Chief Engineer said:

> "There was more than a general awareness of quality control within the organisation, especially amongst the managerial levels. There was an intention to move towards BS5750 certification in the longer term and whilst steps were being taken, in general, towards imposing a quality control system, arising not out of the British Standards, but arising out of the restructuring. The aim was to make the department as competitive with the outside sector as possible. A lot has happened, and it was not appropriate to suddenly jump onto the bandwagon and, especially since there was no immediate need for it. There was nobody saying that they were not going to employ you if you have not got the British Standards accreditation. It was going to be a voluntary

> sort of move, but it is expected to come at
> some time."

To date, that aim or intention to achieve the British Standards accreditation/certification, through a formally recognised quality control system, has not been realised. Many organisations, private and public, that are involved in providing similar types of services have adopted formally recognised quality control systems and have gained the British Standards certification. It seems to me, from recent discussions with present employees that Leeds City Council's Design Consultancy Department intends to achieve such British Standards through partnership with a firm of Private Consultants.

An Architect said:

> "Before restructuring and the introduction
> of the TQM programme, a lot of the
> clients who we could count on as a right
> - Education, Housing, Social Services -
> went off in the opposite direction and got
> private consultants to do the work for them,
> thinking that they will get a better service,
> cheaper. Those client departments are now
> creeping back to us, so we are now getting
> back some of the works which we thought
> we had lost forever."

This statement makes it all the more surprising that the department is now working with a firm of private consultants to increase capacity, as Senior Managers and Politicians put it, rather than recruiting suitable qualified and experienced staff to build the required capacity. May be, they do not expect the present workload to be a long-term position and the partnership is expected to give the organisation that extra flexibility.

Several issues may directly or indirectly affect the quality of the service provided, and this was tested during the interviews. All of the people interviewed, including senior managers, said that political issues affect the quality of their service provision. This is what I expected, since the organisation's reaction and the introduction of the TQM programme was mainly to meet the requirements of CCT, which was a political decision. All of the people interviewed, said that the quality of their service provision is affected by financial issues. This is what I was expecting, because of the existing financial constraints on the organisation and on the client groups serviced by this organisation. These are also political decisions. Some of the people interviewed, said that the quality of their service provision is affected by professional issues. I expected all of those people interviewed to make similar statements since professional institutions set most of the technical guidelines. Therefore, Architects, Assistant Engineers and Engineers are strongly encouraged and are expected to be members of an appropriate professional institution.

In many, if not all, local authority organisations, membership of an appropriate professional organisation or institution is a prerequisite for appointments to the positions of Architects, Assistant Engineers and Engineers.

A summary of the Key Points

Overall, there was a good understanding of the TQM concept.

Expectations vary widely from person to person, and between teams and departments.

Most people felt that there are benefits to be derived from the introduction of the TQM programme for; individuals, the organisation, the client groups and the public.

Most people felt that reorganisation was necessary, and that the methods adopted were the right ones.

Primarily, success is judged on the acceptance of the objectives by senior management and positive feedback from other sources.

Relationships between the various sections are considered to be good. However, the relationship between the organisation and the respective trade unions was poor, but the unions seem to vent their anger towards the politicians rather than the senior managers. This maybe due to the fact that senior managers are also members of trade unions and union leaders are only too aware that in times of conflicts, senior managers have an obligation to minimise the problems that may be caused by such conflicts.

Attitudes towards senior managers did not appear to have changed.

There appears to be strong commitment to the organisation's objectives.

Staff report to more than one supervisor, for example; one member of staff may report to a function head, a project leader and a project co-ordinator. However, all members of staff - except the City Architect - agreed that the role of the co-ordinator is; unspecified, does not work and is unnecessary.

I set out to establish the implications for local authorities implementing a TQM programme. I decided to do this by studying the TQM programme as planned and implemented at the Leeds Design Consultancy, part of the Leeds City Council.

I believed that to meet the requirements of CCT, the TQM programme had to succeed, and that success meant, meeting the objectives those exponents of the TQM concepts claimed would accrue as a result of its successful implementation. In reaching my general conclusion, I have drawn on the evidence from:

1. This study.

2. The British Airways Experience [2].

3. The British Telecom Experience - from interviews and personal experience -.

4. The Nottingham City Council Experience - from interviews and personal experience -.

5. The Barnsley Borough Council Experience - the Council's TQM information pack -.

6. The Westminster City Council Experience - DTI publication -.

7. The Rover Group experience - from visits to Rover and seminars held at the Rover Group -.

The experiences of the organisations listed above are of particular interest, because some have either introduced a TQM programme or have reorganised/restructured in a bid to make those organisations more efficient, and in the case of the City Councils, to meet the requirements of CCT, and have had varying degrees of success.

These organisations were chosen because they provide; stable long-term employment, good pay, pensions and other fringe benefits, which are comparable with Japanese organisations that have introduced TQM programmes and have become competitive and successful.

This work allows some interesting parallels to be drawn with evidence from the study carried out at The Leeds Design Consultancy of Leeds City Council, where the following unfavourable conditions exist:

- Low-trust relationships between engineers and senior management.

- The existence of "us and them" attitudes.

- Authoritative management style.

- Conflict and hostility between politicians and unions.

- Lack of respect between individual employees and between management and other employees.

These contrasting conditions could reasonably be expected to adversely affect the success of the TQM programme being implemented in the Leeds Design Consultancy of Leeds City Council, but my study shows, that whilst these negative conditions contributed to the limitations placed on the success of the TQM programme, they have not adversely affected it to the extent that I anticipated that they would, when I started this study.

According to one Architect:

> "We are doing Business Plans, something that we were not involved with in the past. Because of this we are now looking at what the aspirations of the department are. An annual Business Plan has to be prepared and presented to Council Members. We are all involved when the business plans are being formulated, so you get a feeling of greater involvement. You feel more part of it. When they use that sort of approach, you tend to feel more involved and consequently you become more committed."

Programme Implementation

Strengths

- The TQM programme implementation by the Leeds Design Consultancy followed a fairly orthodox and well-tried pattern. The significant elements in that pattern - the implementation programme's strengths - are:

- Senior Management support, which was visible by their presence at the initial introductory sessions.

- A genuine attempt by senior management and politicians to "sell" the TQM concept through consultation with the various pressure groups within the organisation.

- The appointment of full time management consultants to assist in the development of the TQM programme.

- The allocation of resources, both in terms of man-hours and the necessary financial support, for the implementation of the Performance Related Pay (PRP) associated with the TQM programme.

- The training of all personnel. A significant amount of investment in terms of man-hours and other resources. Although some members of staff argued that, more resources should have been allocated to technical training.

Weaknesses

Unfortunately, for the long-term success of the TQM programme, weaknesses at the implementation stage were to have a far greater impact on the overall success of the TQM programme. Significant weaknesses were:

- The senior people, including the political masters, who were responsible for the introduction of the TQM programme, failed to appreciate the gap that existed between the organisational culture, for example; the management style, the organisational structure, and the underlying principles on which the TQM concept –as discussed earlier – is formed.

- Alienation of the first-line managers. To a large extent, this group is the key to the success of any organisation's TQM programme. Yet, the majority of first-line managers were selected based on their technical ability and not for their ability to lead or manage staff. However, this seems to be normal practice for this type of organisation where all employees are expected to be very well qualified academically, highly skilled and well motivated.

- Trying to do too much too quickly. There were too many other programmes going on or being introduced at the same time, for example; the change of location that caused a lot of conflicts with staff and associated unions, restructuring to reduce staffing levels due to the reduction in projects from client groups, changes in technical requirements to meet the increasing public demands for higher standards etc. If the organisation had allowed the influences to staff attitudes, caused by all these things happening together, to settle down to a greater extent before the TQM programme was introduced, then, perhaps the TQM programme would have stood a greater chance of succeeding.

- Failing to identify the lack of support for the TQM concept amongst employees. The employers - politicians and senior managers - in my view were insensitive towards their employees' attitudes and feelings. At this point in time there were so many changes taking place within the organisation and external to it, over a very short period, and members of staff felt threatened. They – employees - were well aware that, due to some of these changes, some of them were going to lose their jobs. They were also aware that senior managers had no control over some of the changes, which were forced on the organisation because of changes in client groups and public demands together with changes in client groups funding strategies etc. A number of employees fail to support the TQM concept because they felt that senior managers should, at that stage, have been concentrating on managing those changes over which they - senior managers - had no control rather than introducing changes that they – employees - felt could have been introduced at a later date. If the organisation had been more sensitive to this problem, then, perhaps the TQM programme would not have gone ahead.

Perhaps the biggest weakness, in view of the previous point, was the organisation not starting with a pilot scheme. A clear indication that there would be a pilot scheme for a prescribed period would have reduced employees' hostilities, the possibility of a larger scale failure and the accusation of "flavour of the month management techniques".

Have these weaknesses affected the outcome of the TQM programme? I believe they have. The rapid, initial growth of the programme could have lead to a complete programme failure during the early stages of its implementation. The lack of support and the alienation of the first-line managers and supervisors was one of the main ingredients that lead to a partial stagnation, which was to ultimately affect the long-term viability of the TQM programme.

Leeds Design Consultancy's programme of implementation had a substantial number of flaws. Some examples of these were:

- The whole of Leeds City Council was not involved in the TQM programme so the client groups, who bid each year for funds for future City Council's and community projects, and to whom Leeds Design Consultancy provides its services, did not buy into the TQM programme.

- Key groups on whom the success of the TQM programme depended were alienated, for example, first-line managers and supervisors.

- The organisation was insensitive to; the feelings, apprehensions, and attitudes of junior members of staff.

- The management style was too autocratic and machine-like, and required substantial changes/ modifications before the implementation of a TQM programme.

These flaws, together with the hostile environment into which the TQM concept was introduced, had the effect of limiting the overall effectiveness of the TQM programme. However, some measurable benefits have accrued. For example:

- Significant resources allocated to staff training.

- The allocation of financial resources in support of the PRP implementation.

- Staffs say; "we are doing Business Plans and we are looking at what the aspirations of the department are".

- A number of client groups - the departments of Housing, Education, and Social Services -, who had previously taken their services to private organisations, have returned their services to Leeds Design Consultancy.

• Employees are more committed to satisfying the organisation's customers.

If in all aspects of their work, employees are committed to promoting the organisation's objectives - and all of those with whom I spoke said they are -, they will ensure equal access to and promote good relations between all sections of the community and client groups. To do this they will have to; maintain and monitor the standards of all services provided, provide quality services to all client groups and the public, ensure that individuals do not suffer through lack of knowledge of the services available to them, and exercise a responsible influence on the development of City Council policies and services throughout the City of Leeds.

In all areas and situations where mistakes have been made or performance has faltered, managers should develop strategies that would ensure lessons are learnt and applied for the future benefit of the organisation. Such mistakes should provide an opportunity for learning and a means of improving personal and organisational performance.

Before the TQM programme was introduced, the organisation should have installed formal quality systems that could be checked or reviewed, on a regular basis, through accreditation to a formal quality system. Over fifteen years ago, it was the BS5750 system, but over the years it has developed into the ISO 9002 system and more recently the ISO 9001:2000 standard. Under the quality system the organisation's services can be monitored continuously, through internal reviews and checked by external inspections. The accreditation could be completely re-assessed once every three years, to judge how well the systems are working. Quality accreditation would ensure that the organisation's work is carried out to the highest possible standard.

Working Relationships

Evidence from the interviews suggests that working relationships have improved. However, this improvement was not sustained and there appear to be a low-trust situation in day-to-day relationships. This was particularly apparent to the first-line managers, who found it difficult to reconcile the change. There are a number of possible explanations for this resistance to change:

1. Pressure from other trade union members, who were not involved in the TQM programme, to conform to attitudes and patterns of behaviour that existed prior to the introduction of the TQM programme. These were the same attitudes and patterns of behaviour that the TQM programme was expected to modify.

2. A temporary improvement brought about through an unusual amount of attention from senior management - a sort of mini "Hawthorn Effect" -.

3. The view held by many trade unions' supporters was that PRP undermines the ethics of equal pay.

According to one Engineer:

> "I applied for a regarding; I do not trust the Head of Building Services so I made my application to the City Architect."

Although the majority of those people interviewed said that PRP was good for the organisation and it was working well, the above statement would suggest otherwise. If PRP was working in the way that it was intended, this regarding issue should have been picked up during that member of staff's annual review associated with PRP. It may be that due to the early retirement of the previous Head of Building Services - who was instrumental in the introduction of the TQM and PRP programmes -, and the new Head of Building Services, recruited from another local authority, had no interest in either TQM or PRP, and this problem was not teased out at his recruitment interview.

According to another Engineer:

> "Our new Head of Building Services do not care much about solving customer's problems. He wants us to stay in the office and just design, design and let other people solve the problems. He is different from the last Head, he is flash, and likes to be seen with the right people. He is career minded; he is single minded and not the sort of person you can trust. I enjoyed working with the old Head of Building Services. You could go to him with your problems but you can't with this chap."

Whilst relationships within Leeds Design Consultancy improved, relationships with trade union members from other City Council departments worsened. The findings from this study suggests that TQM "success" may involve trade-off in heightened tension and potential conflict between employees, and raise the possibility that employee resistance may constrain the implementation of TQM initiatives.

Evidence from my study suggests that this problem may extend further and exhibit itself in a number of ways, for example, causing some members to request transfers to other departments – effectively changing camps - and others to resign and seek appointments with private organisations.

In the light of the above statements, I feel that it is of the utmost importance that when an organisation is considering the introduction of a TQM programme, a holistic approach should be taken. That is. TQM programmes should involve the complete organisation, not just one department or section or group. This piecemeal approach was doomed from the start.

One Senior Architect said:

> "Because so many people left, they had to get new people but they were interesting people who had no local government experience. This did not make any sense because they were not familiar with the procedures and it was difficult for them to slot in."

I was always very sceptical of professional people leaving private industry or organisations to join local authority organisations, because the financial rewards and other benefits, for the same type of work, is usually much higher in the private industry.

Another problem that Leeds Design Consultancy could face is; recruiting a large number of new professional people from private industry may jeopardise the TQM programme - since they had not bought into it -, and customers may suffer until the new people become fully acquainted with local government procedures. However, the organisation may well benefit from recruiting new professional people because they could be selected depending of their views towards the programmes and changes being implemented.

Was TQM a Success for LDC?

According to the City Architect, his concept of quality does not follow exactly as outlined in the manuals or the theories of the quality gurus; he said:

> "I worked it out for myself, there are several benefits. Customer satisfaction is my principal aim with services fit for their purpose, reliability, good value and delivery on time. It is only common sense."

Quality, price and service, he argued, were what made people come back for more.

Put in this context, the TQM programme seems to be successful because, although there are some disagreements amongst existing employees, in respect of some of the approaches adopted, there are general agreement that customers are involved with all projects in a way that they have not been involved before the TQM programme was implemented, and that the aim at all times is to satisfy the customer.

All interviewees agreed that the organisation's customers/ client groups such as the departments of; Social Services, Leisure Services and Education, who, prior to the introduction of the TQM programme into LDC, had taken some of their work to other organisations, are now taking all of their work to LDC. A recent customer survey carried out by LDC has shown that its customers are satisfied with the services being provided.

LDC now has a new City Architect who was a Senior Architect with LDC when the TQM programme was implemented. In a recent discussion with the new City Architect, he did not mention the TQM programme, but he made the following statement:

> "Since you left us we have gone through quite a lot of changes including change of location. For example; we have changed from LDC to The Leeds Design Services Agency, then we became Architectural Design Services Development Department and combined with Planning and Highways Design. We have now formed a Strategic Design Alliance, this is a partnership with Jacobs a private firm of consultants. This Strategic Design Alliance is to deliver the very best architectural services for future developments across the City of Leeds. I have been involved with the management of so many changes now, that I class myself as an expert in Change Management. I think that we are doing very well but I want the other Leeds City Council's departments to follow our lead. The City of Leeds spends over £200m each year and there are no proper planning for this spends. The priorities seem to depend on the Council Members who could shout loudest. I have managed so many changes, successfully, and I would like to extend my expertise throughout the whole of Leeds City Council, in respect of

> setting priorities for how that public money
> is spent."

The above statement, by the new City Architect, is rather surprising, because one of the main reasons for introducing; the TQM programme, together with the restructuring and the associated early retirements, redeployments and redundancies, was so that LDC could successfully compete with private organisations. Now with a new head and one who was involved with the TQM implementation, LDC – or under its new heading "Architectural Design Services Development Department" – has formed a partnership with a private firm of consultants. This partnership is expected to enhance the capacity and responsiveness of Leeds City Council's Design and Development Services, by combining public and private consultancy experience. You may call me a pessimist, but I cannot help wondering if this partnership had anything to do with the change in political majority on the Leeds City Council. It also may be that they see this as the least painful way of dealing with rapid capacity changes that takes place in local authority organisations, as a result of continuous internal and external environmental changes.

The projects for which finance have been committed and awarded to LDC, shows that the organisation is well placed to survive any threats from competition over the next 4 to 5 years, but the organisation could do better by address the following areas.

Communication Strategy

When the various changes were announced, the organisation had no communication strategy in place so that members of staff could be properly informed about; the changes, the reasons for those changes and what effect the changes would have on the organisation and themselves. Whilst members of staff were living and working through the changes, it was not clear to the majority of them, why the changes were initiated in the first place. It is important that before change in any organisation is initiated that senior managers give careful thought to how that change will be communicated to staff. The following are some ideas that may help organisations with their communication of change strategy.

Communication aims to:

1. Explain to all members of staff the reason for the change.

2. Win staff commitment, confidence and trust in respect of the change.

3. Alleviate staff fears and resistance to the change.

4. Inform staff of the benefits of the change for the organisation and themselves.

5. Outline to staff what is involved and what they could expect.

6. Provide staff with opportunities to raise any concerns that they may have and encourage them to give honest feedback.

Good Communication Strategy

The following are some ideas that will help facilitate good communications to changes within an organisation:

- Managers should ensure that they have knowledge of how their failure to communicate effectively could seriously damage the success of the change process.

- Managers should know the priorities of the stakeholders – in this case; the elected members, the client groups, employees and the public.

- Managers should have some idea of the messages to be sent to stakeholders.

- Delivery mechanisms for these messages will need to be specified, for example, the methods or channels that will be used to deliver the messages.

- Feedback from stakeholders is essential; therefore, mechanisms must be put in place to facilitate such feedback.

- Systems must be put in place to respond quickly to issues and concerns raised by stakeholders during the communication process.

- Communications systems and processes must be reviewed regularly and updated if necessary.

- There should be repetition of the messages by the use of several communication sources and actions taken to reinforce the words of the message.

- It is difficult and sometimes impossible to re-establish credibility of a previously inaccurate or misleading source of information, it is therefore important, to establish and maintain the integrity of the information sources.

- Ensure that representatives of all stakeholders attend communications meetings, so that they may receive firsthand, information and documentations. In this case, all communicators must be; confident, capable and be positive about the process.

- If only one communications meeting is held, some stakeholders may not be able to attend because of work commitments. Therefore, it is important that the same communications meeting should be run several times so that all stakeholders can attend. People should be given enough time to discuss and respond to the information.

- It is good practise to re-enforce the information given in the meetings by giving all those attending written summaries, especially answers to questions.

- People should be told of target dates in the decision-making and implementation process, even if it is just to reaffirm previous information because, it is less stressful for people to deal with uncertainty if they are regularly updated.

- Regular updates that summarise; the main issues, achievements and progress to date, problems that have been overcome, and any positive outcomes will all help to dispel rumours.

- Good communications strategy that keeps everyone well informed would drastically reduce the levels of any rumours that may arise. Feedback sessions and face-to-face contacts would provide a good opportunity to deal with any rumours, as soon as they start to surface.

- Managers must ensure that all messages are prepared and agreed, so that only correct information is given. They must also make sure that all stakeholders receive the information, through the communications process. This should include members of staff who may be absent through holidays or illness.

Quality procedures

There are no formal quality systems in place, so there are no systems procedures, written or otherwise. This leads to duplication of activities throughout the organisation, and people are using different procedures to provide similar services, even when they are working to the same line-manager or supervisor. The setting up of a formal quality system, with properly documented procedures, would eliminate this waste.

An organisation's success depends on its ability to deliver great service, and to do that, it relies heavily on the efforts of all its people. Since achieving success is due to the efforts of everyone in the organisation, the calibre and energy of all the company's employees will also be an important factor in achieving that success. The culture in the organisation is also very important. Ideally, the organisation's culture should be customer focus and together with service obsession, should be top of the organisation's agenda.

A Framework to Maintain Standards

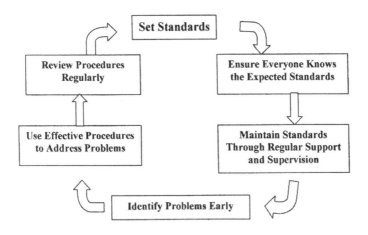

Probably the most effective method of preventing complaints, from customers, because of poor service quality plus disciplinary and grievance issues in the organisation, is setting out the expected standards of work required and the expected standards of behaviour, in the workplace and in contacts with clients/customers. Unfortunately, many organisations, including Leeds City Council, assumes that everyone understands the expected standards, simply because they work their. The standards are often implicit and not always explained, in detail or open for discussion, between management and other employees. In addition to this, managers in technical organisations, such as Leeds Design Consultancy, tends to give up some of their managerial authority or standards setting, to the professional institutions to which those employees belong. In most cases, this failing, only comes to light when a problem needs to be sorted out.

Some of the difficulties in establishing standards of performance, may be identified simply, by asking a group of managers or team leaders, "what makes good quality of service" and listen to the wide range of responses. To establish acceptable standards is not always easy, because the organisation have to decide, in advance of carrying out the work or service, what is "good quality", and use this as the benchmark. Leeds Design Consultancy have certain standards, that are set through employees membership of appropriate professional institutions, never-the-less, within these standards, the organisation's own standards will influence what individuals consider to be good enough, but individuals should always refer to the organisation's guidance, for current good practice.

Some of the things that may help to set standards will be to establish the range of tasks that are necessary for each job, and the experience, skills, qualifications and attitudes needed to carry out those tasks. These can be found in the job descriptions and competences. Competences describe what someone has to be able to do in a particular role. They also describe the underpinning skills, knowledge and behaviour required. Therefore, they provide a framework within which staff and managers can assess performance.

Training

The system exists that would identify training needs – PRP -, although it is not used, but no system exist to address the training needs. Because of this lack of training, IT equipments are not fully utilised. Over £859,000.00 was spent in providing the most up-to-date state of the art equipments, however, due to lack of training resources, approximately 80% of the equipment is not utilised. This is also an area of extreme waste because, if employees were properly trained in the operation of the various equipments that were available, then Leeds Design Consultancy's efficiency would be greatly improved. The most economical way of addressing this problem, is to, train a small core of employees and set up an IT section. Engineers and Architects could then produce design sketches from which the IT section would produce working drawings. This would reduce the time that Engineers and Architects spent on the drawing boards thus leaving Engineers and Architects time for more professional and technical demanding work.

Overall, the TQM programme seems to have achieved its organisational objectives of greater employee involvement as well as changing the attitudes and working culture of staff and managers. Employees are more involved in discussions with customers/clients at all stages of their projects, to ensure that customers are satisfied with the services being provided. This did not happen before the introduction of the TQM programme. In the past, Engineers and Architects would do their designs for a project, obtain the necessary funds, complete the work and then hand over the completed project to the customer, without consultation. Employees are working to the targets that have been set and although in some cases the targets are not properly negotiated with staff, employees are committed to those targets, to the extent that they take work home in an effort to meet those targets. Before the introduction of the TQM programme, employees who were not managers, did not concern themselves with targets. They were also not concerned with meeting their projects' completion dates. These gross organisational failings were generally accepted, by managers and politicians alike.

In my view, although Leeds Design Consultancy have made considerable progress in enhancing its performance and efficiency, it is difficult to see, how improvements in one department, could make significant improvements - if any -, to one of the largest local authority in the UK. Greater efficiency would have been achieved, if the whole of Leeds

City Council were involved in the TQM programme, with the programme being driven from the top and the Chief Executive taking the lead.

Consensus in Local Government

Leeds Design Consultancy has the opportunity to forge strong working relationships with other Leeds City Council departments and the public and to develop a broad consensus about the aims of the organisation. It is expected to set budgets at a level that the fees from client departments can sustain, in a period when client departments are having severe restrictions, put on both their capital and revenue expenditures.

From my study of the organisation and an in-depth interview, of one and a half hours, with the City Architect, Leeds Design Consultancy's vision of quality, gives consideration as to how best to encourage the effective delivery of high quality services. This, the study shows have been achieved, through restructuring and the introduction of a TQM programme. This seems to be in line with what other organisations, which are facing similar changes to their external and internal environments, are doing or have done. Some of these organisations are; Westminster City Council, Barnsley City Council, Nottingham City Council, British Telecom, British Airways, Leicester City Council, The Rover Group and many others. However, they have not all had the same level of success.

Forming partnerships, in my view is a good idea, however, I have difficulties reconciling or looking favourably on partnerships between groups with different aims and objectives. I have difficulties reconciling the partnership between one group, whose objective should maximising value for money and best quality of service provision, for the public, with a private group whose objective is, to maximise profits for its shareholders. You may want to make reference to partnerships through privately financed schemes or projects, but you should not get confused with these two types of partnerships, because they are not similar. In the case of the partnership between Leeds Design Consultancy and the firm of Private Consultants, this partnership is for the spending of public money that are already in the City Council's budget, for that financial accounting period, associated with already approved projects. In the case of the other partnerships, which is also taking place in many other local authority organisations through the UK, the private firms or organisations are providing the finance/money for projects, that otherwise, would not get off the ground, without such partnerships. The private firms or organisations expect to make profits from these partnerships but local authority feel that they and the public are benefiting from these partnerships in two major ways:

1. Without these privately financed initiatives, some of those very costly capital programmes, such as; new schools and hospitals might never have got off the ground.

2. It is argued that the profits gained by those partnership organisations, for their capital, is far less than the interest that the local authority would have had to pay, if it had to borrow the money to finance those capital programmes/projects.

I feel that seeking partnerships with the Architect's Departments of other local authority organisations would have created a much better partnership for Leeds Design Consultancy. This type of partnership, with other local authority organisations, would help these partnership organisations to manage the organisational changes, caused by changes in their external and internal environments. In so doing, they would deliver the best quality services to their customers - clients and the public -, because they would be able to take up the slack that occurs form time to time in such organisations. Taking up operational slack within these organisations, would reap benefits for all organisations involved in the partnership, in terms of:

- Providing best value for money, for clients and the public, through the economies of scale that these partnerships would create.

- Since their objectives are more or less similar, in terms of customer satisfaction and not for profit operation, they would be able to share; best practice designs, operations and management techniques for quality operations, without feeling the need to compete with each other.

- Members of staff would gain wider experience because they would be involved with more varied projects, which in turn, would make their work more interesting.

- Members of staff, including managers and team leaders, would become better motivated because of the variations in their work and interactions with other professionals in similar organisations.

One Architect said:

"I do not know who thought of this partnership with a private firm. There is only one winner in our situation and that is the private firm. I cannot see what benefit the City Council is getting out of it. At one time we would commission consultants to do certain works but they had to compete for that work and we were in charge and we called the shots. The case we have now is; a private firm that does not have to compete for the work that they do and to me and some other colleagues, they seem to be getting the more lucrative jobs. They also seem to be calling the shots. I am sure that the senior managers would say something different but other people feel like I do. The private firm is only in it for the profit, they are not interested in satisfying the public, like we do, and when things go wrong and the public are unhappy, it is us, the City Council employees, who gets the flack from the public and the politicians."

It would seem, from this statement that some members of staff are far from happy or satisfied with the public and private organisations' partnership arrangements. There also seems to be the suggestion that this partnership arrangement, and the way it operates, is restricting the professional development of members of staff who are employed in the public sector organisation -Leeds Design Consultancy -.

The reader would have seen an earlier statement of a discussion with the present/new City Architect, in which he is suggesting, that the City Council's priorities should be set or be determined by City Council's Managers/Officers and that, with his vast experience of managing change, he is well placed to take the lead in that area. Well to me that sounds rather strange to hear such a very Senior Manager of the City Council suggesting that the City Council's Employees - and not the Political Members who are elected by the public - should be setting the City Council's priorities. It seems to me that what is lacking here is, political awareness, and I feel that public sector managers, especially senior managers, must be able to manage with political awareness, if they are going to be successful in providing the best quality services for the public.

Internal Control and Risk Management

A Board – made up of senior managers – should be responsible for the organisation's systems of internal control and for reviewing its effectiveness. The system should be designed to manage, rather than eliminate, the risk of failure to achieve the organisation's objectives. It should provide reasonable and not absolute assurance against misstatement, misunderstanding or loss. The concept of reasonable assurance recognises that the cost of control procedures should not exceed the benefits.

The organisation should have; dedicated resource to embed processes and controls across the whole organisation. It should operate a number of additional self-assessment exercises, which includes monthly certification of compliance with key operational and financial control systems. There should also be an annual control self-assessment exercise that requires managers to assess the effectiveness of; the organisation's fundamental operating controls over all aspects of its operations, in addition to any other financial controls, that are covered by the organisation's Financial Controls Toolkit. The results of this exercise should be used by Internal Audit when planning its work for the forthcoming year.

Training

A proper and formal course of training for public sector managers is needed. Such a course should give these managers, the necessary skills that are needed, to manage the political dimension of the public services that they are task with providing. The course/training should make significant contributions, to the understanding of the relevance and importance of political skills in the workplace. I am certain that this type of training will generate further insights, into, how such skills can be constructively developed and deployed in practice.

British Airways Experience

The Senior Management team of British Airways' Technical workshops formed the view, in the late 1987, that a TQM programme would assist them in improving their contribution to British Airways' success. In order to be the best in the business, the Management Team at British Airways Technical Workshops, decided that they have to win through; teamwork, customer satisfaction, profitability and reputation. They also believed that, if British Airways was going to continue to be a world-class organisation that could beat the best of the competition, then, the strategies and processes adopted by the Management Team, must create a vision that would inspire British Airways employees and gain their commitment, and that this could be achieved through TQM. It was also felt that TQM would not just continue to create interest in the organisation, from some of the best university graduates, but it would help to stem the tide of discontent amongst existing staff and customer dissatisfaction.

Along the route to TQM the following key stages have been identified:

1. Carry out a diagnostic survey of the current position within Technical Workshops and report the findings.

2. Obtain full support and commitment to the concept of TQM, from all levels of management and respond positively to the outcomes of the diagnostic report.

3. Educate all staff in the principles of TQM and facilitate the necessary changes in management style.

4. Produce changes in policies, procedures and work practices that would fit and facilitate the required new organisational culture.

5. Begin the process of quality improvements.

6. Review the progress made and encourages a sustained commitment from all levels of the organisation.

The diagnostic survey was made on two broad fronts. In order to examine the issues and problems facing staff, a survey was carried out, across the total population of the Technical Workshops, and customer and supply areas. In addition to this, managers wanted to determine the cost of not getting it right first time, and to identify areas of waste. To achieve this, an analysis of the cost of quality was performed.

The approach adopted, in the collection of quality costs, was, to breakdown the quality-related activities of the staff into three main areas:

1. Prevention – activities that ensure "right first time" performance.

2. Appraisal – activities that check whether "right first time" is being achieved.

3. Failure – activities that result from not performing "right first time".

Each manager or team leader was asked to make an assessment, of the way in which their staff spent time on quality-related activities. Knowledge of how quality costs are incurred has been of considerable benefit in the education of staff on the concept and principles of TQM. It has also helped to justify and reinforce the need for TQM training to; overcome any scepticism towards TQM, promote considerable debate on the subject of TQM, and to ensure that the work of individual improvement projects can be measured.

The information collected from the diagnostic survey was put into a diagnostic report and identified seven areas for improvement:

1. Employees' view of management.

2. Management style.

3. Implementing changes.

4. Communication.

5.   Systems and procedures.

6.   Facilities and conditions.

7.   Employee attitudes.

A series of three-day courses for managers were held. These courses explained the concept and philosophy of TQM and outlined the findings of the diagnostic report. Managers, at all levels, were encouraged to put forward ideas and action plans, for the involvement of their staff in the improvement process. To achieve this and be successful required some changes to the style of management.

Similar courses were held for all employees. The delegates for each course were taken from various areas of the Workshops, to facilitate an exchange of ideas across all departments.

Quality Improvement Groups, each involving up to 12 people, set about actively pursuing improvement projects. Examples of these projects, includes; improved methods of storing aircraft test equipments, to ensure ease of location and control of certification, an improved library facility for storage of approved technical publications and design of new workshop performance measures to ensure meaningful and easily understood performance figures.

British Airways Technical Workshops were totally committed to the idea of being recognised as the best in the business as seen by its customers, competitors as well as by all managers and staff of British Airways.

BA's the TQM programme was launched in September 1988 and by the end of 1999 the benefits of that TQM programme was already beginning to show through; benefits such as:

- Better communication between staff and between staff and supervisors/managers across all departments.

- Improved team working.

- Shorter turnaround times, for aircrafts, during servicing and maintenance.

- Reduction in time lost due to staff illness.

- Improved attendance figures.

- Just-in-time delivery of parts and equipments, due mainly to improved relationships, with parts and equipments manufacturers.

- Reduction in the cost of storage of parts and equipments.

- Improved efficiency, throughout all departments.

- Employees in all departments took more pride in the standard and quality of their work and also of their appearance.

Positive changes have also taken place, in the top-level measures, which are used to report progress to the directorate. These measures include, the percentage of components with a positive serviceable stock hording, number of unserviceable units in the workshop, and the number of units produced per month.

By the end of 1991 conditions at British Airways, as seen by its customers and shareholders, had improved to such an extent that, it was argued that British Airways was one of the classic turnaround stories of that period. To raise the quality of the service it offered together with year-on year increased profits and dividends, it had to undertake a wide range of changes, from new livery to extensive training and reorganising of jobs, to bring more people closer to the customer. Those changes were based on the requirements of the TQM programme together with extensive market research, which identified the standard of service that customers expected, from a major international airline, such as British Airways.

British Airways Standards Drop

In 1987, when British Airways Workshops launched its TQM programme, the company faced very little competition, on many of the routes that it served and was provided with some of the best slots in the UK's Heathrow airport. This period was just before privatisation; British Airways faced little or no competition for routes into and out of the UK and controlled the major share of the UK domestic market. Since the company as a whole was not involved or committed to the TQM programme, I cannot, with hand on heart, say that all this progress was due to the TQM programme implementation.

During this period, there were other things happening within the organisation, which I feel, was about the organisation positioning itself for privatisation; the infrastructure was improved, staff numbers were reduced, the introduction of new marketing information and uniforms, large investment in control systems and terminal facilities, the replacement of some 60% of its aircrafts, the introduction of computerised reservations and a competitive pricing structure that made it very difficult for competitors to compete or to enter the competition. However, all of these areas and functions were not part of the TQM programme.

British Airways adopted a ruthless strategy against its competitors, but I cannot say that all the strategies were above board. Shared booking information systems were developed, as a way of helping the customers of all airlines, however, in the early 1990s, it was suggested, by some commentators, that British Airways used that information to encourage Virgin customers to transfer to British Airways, by giving those customers false information. This resulted in British Airways being taken to court and was find £3 million costs and over £600,000 damages. Although questions were raised as to how much the Chairman and the Chief Executive knew about these activities, together with criticisms, that such problems was due to the culture change within British Airways, these were not part of the TQM programme.

Although much of British Airways turnaround can be attributed to the TQM programme, launched by its workshops, some of the turnaround could be attributed to other factors, such as, the company's cultural transformation. However, all areas of the company did not commit to the TQM programme, as the workshops did, but instead, pursued cultural change through influence and control of employees'; norms, attitudes, thoughts and values. Employees in areas other than the workshops, became very hostile to this new style of management and any co-operation that existed between staff and management was due mainly to; employees' ambition and pride in their work and not due to their belief in the company. In this period, it seems to me that employees did not trust managers and managers did not trust employees. British Airways "new management" styles were introduced differently in the different departments, which resulted in many conflicts between employees and management. By 1995, when British Airways culture change was seen as a resounding success, at least one group or department each year was having industrial dispute.

Conflict at British Airways

By 1994, at a time when British Airways was making profits that was far in excess of market expectations, top managers were demonstrating indifference to the TQM programme. Since top managers were reporting major successes in British Airways Workshops and suggesting that they were due mainly to the successful implementation of the TQM programme, one would expect that, the next logical step would have been to improve on that success, by introducing the TQM programme to all areas of the company's operations, but the organisation failed to grasp that opportunity and instead, embarked on a number of changes, which not only undo the TQM programme of the Workshops, but created a lot of conflicts in other departments as well as the Workshops. Some of the changes were:

- British Airways made agreements, with other major airlines, that created a system of terms and conditions, which saw employees at major airports given privileges that were not available to employees at regional airports.

- British Airways introduced; sub-contract, part-time and seasonal working to most of its operations.

- Some operations, such as, data processing, were relocated.

- Some parts of the Workshops, such as, the engine overhaul department, were sold.

- Employees, who were employed in the departments/ operations that were sold or merged with partners or associates, did not enjoy the same benefits as those who remain with British Airways core operations.

- British Airways staff, no longer felt secure in their jobs and although the organisation made every effort to develop a new culture, based on certain types of work ethics and behaviour, employees felt that the organisation's employment policies and practices, had nothing to do with the new culture.

During 1997, British Airways tried to change the payment structure for its cabin staff, but the proposal met with fierce resistance and although the company gave a guarantee, that over a three year period, under the new payment system, no cabin crew staff would earn less than they were presently earning, cabin crew staff felt that the proposal was purely about saving money. All negotiations around the proposal for changing the payment structure for cabin crew staff, failed.

The above changes brought about some hostile reactions from employees that were not welcomed by British Airways. Employees had doubts and serious concerns about the changes, which resulted in a large number of representations and continuous disputes, even at the time when British Airways was claiming that the changes were successful. This high rate of conflict continued throughout this period up to the end of the 1990s.

By the end of the year 2000, British Airways was predicting huge increase in profits. However, much of that predicted profit was to be achieved, through savings from large-scale redundancies, with some vacancies being filled by recruiting

R. Ashley Rawlins TD. DL.

employees on lower pay. In addition to this, British Airways formed partnerships with charter airlines, as well as continuing to outsource some of its activities/operations, to other operators.

Industrial Action at British Airways

By the year 2000, British Airways had spent an enormous amount of money, time and effort training its managers and although that training, which took place over a very long period of some fifteen to sixteen years, was aimed at changing the organisation's management culture, to one of caring and putting people first, it was not part of the TQM programme, which by this stage was long forgotten. The money, time and effort spent on that management training, for British Airways managers, was wasted, because despite all that training, bullying of staff continued, even when there were threats of industrial actions. Rather than finding a solution to the problem, by possibly extending the TQM programme to all departments, employees were informed that if they took industrial action, they might lose certain staff privileges, such as; pension rights, staff discounts, promotion prospects, face disciplinary action, be dismissed and even be sued for damages. Despite these threats, in 1997, British Airways employees, voted overwhelmingly in favour of strike action but as a result of the above threats, only about 250 employees declared that they were officially on strike whilst about 2,250 employees telephoned to report that they were ill. British Airways' style of management failed, because despite the company's threats, the action took the form of mass illness, which caused most of its flights to be cancelled.

British Airways managers seems very reluctant to learn from their mistakes because over the last ten years, none of its

198

top managers have been able to solve a problem, that is as fundamental as, pay and conditions, and now in early 2007, British Airways employees, have voted overwhelmingly, in favour of strike action because negotiations on pay and working conditions have failed.

It seems to me that British Airways would have been more prudent if it had pursued its "culture change" by extending its TQM programme that was reported as a success story for its Workshops, to include the whole organisation, instead of selling off the group that found success through TQM. Its top management was short-sighted in their pursuit of quick but short-term profit. By 2002, British Airways share price, was at its lowest level since privatisation and I believe that it was due mainly to poor management. However, British Airways blamed the loss of value, on the stock market and more specific, on the collapse of the market as a whole, rather than agree that its lack of performance was due to poor management and lack of leadership.

In 2004, British Airways reviewed its procedures to provide clearer instructions and clearly define the role of each engineer. Maintenance staff also changed their procedures for serving engine oil, to prevent over-filling. This came about, because the company received recommendations from the AAIB, which identified factors in British Airways' maintenance process that led to an incident in late 2003. In the mid 1990s, British Airways employed about 9,500 engineers and maintenance staff but by 2003 that figure had reduced to about 6,000 and its fleet remains at a similar size to what it was in 1995. However, if the TQM programme was still in place, that incident may not have occurred, since the continuous review of procedures and processes is an integral part of any TQM programme.

By July 2007, despite earlier promises by BA that the problems with baggage handling was under control, the problem was getting worse, according to BA's staff at Heathrow Airport. They said:

> "The back-log of baggage that has not arrived at customers' destination is so great that bags are being driven in Lorries from Heathrow Airport to Italy for sorting."

This problem is causing stress amongst BA's customers, who have missed; weddings, graduation ceremonies, and other family celebrations. BA has turned its back on its TQM programme that was so successful and seems to have lost all control over its systems. BA, it seems, is also failing in the IT stakes, for example; the organisation is encouraging customers to book their BA flights online, I recently made such a booking but it took; over two weeks, forty plus telephone calls, and waiting up to thirty minutes, on the telephone, for a BA agent to answer my call. The usual reply here was; "sorry! I cannot help you; I do not know anything about the system." This demonstrate to me that BA could solve most of its problem by re-implementing its TQM programme, but this time, the programme should be implemented throughout the whole organisation and not just one department, as before.

British Airways' Attempts at Salvaging

British Airways attempted to address the above problems by putting more emphasis on managing the organisation's culture, mainly through training sessions for its staff, together with question and answer seminars held with groups of employees. This training was very expensive and not cost effective because it produced few positive reactions from staff. Staff moral never recovered completely, after the various industrial actions, which cost the company in excess of £130 million, and profits also suffered badly. By the year 2000, British Airways was reporting losses in excess of £240 million and with such poor performance; the company was kept out of the red only by disposing of some of its assets. Nevertheless, its share price took a tumble, a reflection of the market's lack of confidence in the organisation.

Despite British Airways' efforts to change the culture of the organisation, industrial actions still threatens the company in the year 2007. In January 2007, Cabin Crews voted in favour of strike action because they were dissatisfied with their conditions of pay and sick leave entitlement. After lengthy discussions, between British Airways and the respective unions of the Cabin Crews, the proposed strike action was called off. However, by February 2007, more than 4,000 British Airways' employees were threatening to take industrial action – in the form of strikes - over proposed changes to British Airways' pension scheme.

On the 13th February 2007, British Airways, inconvenienced and upset a large number of its customers, when it said that customers could book-in only one piece of baggage without having to pay excess baggage charges, irrespective of the weight. The company stated that this change was mainly for health and safety reasons. I think, that statement was nonsense and made without thinking. Surely, one large heavy baggage is more a health and safety risk than two small baggages, with combined weights equalling that of the one large baggage. It seems to me that this decision was British Airways' reaction to the loss of customers' baggage, after disruptions to flights, due to bad weather conditions in January 2007. If British Airways had continued with its TQM programme and rolled it out to the whole organisation, then it would have systems and procedures in place to deal with such problems, as part of the TQM programme.

Over the last fifteen years, none of British Airways' managers have been able to solve a problem as fundamental as pay and conditions. It seems to me that British Airways would have been more prudent, to have pursued its culture change by extending its TQM programme to the whole organisation instead of selling off the group that found success through the implementation of a TQM programme. Top management were short-sighted in pursuing short term profit because despite the disposal of assets, by the year 2002 the company's share price was at its lowest since privatisation, which I believe was due to poor management, however, British Airways blamed the company's loss of value on the collapse of the market as a whole, but I believe that the lack of performance was due to poor management and lack of leadership.

By March 2007, although British Airways stated that it had reached agreements with employees and their respective unions, regarding the company's pensions problems/deficit – the price of British Airways' shares increased from £4.12 to £5.25 per share, within two weeks following the report in which that statement was made, showing the effect of that report on market confidence – but one union representing 4,500 British Airways employees – mainly ground staff – insists that the pensions problems was still very much alive and was threatening strike action during Easter 2007. Other unions, representing the majority of the company's employees, have agreed to the new pensions plan, but the union representing some of British Airways' lowest-paid workers said that they have rejected the offer because it is unfair to its members. Union representatives said: "The statement of agreement is untrue. We have agreed to recommend the proposals to our members. The company's management is still awaiting the outcome of a ballot by our members and if our members choose to reject our recommendation, then, our strike threat is still real." So it would seem that at this stage, British Airways still has a long way to go in securing acceptance of its pensions proposals. It is also clear to me that by the end of February 2007, the company is still demonstrating some communications problems. This problem would not occur if the TQM programme was rolled out to include the whole organisation. Another problem is the fragmented union representation. Staff consultation would be better served if all employees were represented by one union because it seems to me that the unions are competing with each other, rather than seeking what is best for their members.

I also believe that these problems could be overcome by putting more effort into the following:

- Effective management training that would give managers the authority and tools to correct most quality problems.

- Management should plan for the future and be able to foresee problems that could cause manpower wastage.

- The organisation should work at improving the quality of every element of the business, from planning to service delivery. This includes; all services, people relationships, attention to customers' needs, shareholders, and management approaches.

- The company should develop systems that would improve communications between departments and between managers and other employees as well as between the company and its customers. Such systems should support the automatic sharing of good practices between departments.

- There should be company-wide quality control.

With company-wide quality control in place, one should see the following taking place:

- The quality of services provided should improve and problems and complaints reduced.

- Service reliability will improve.

- There will be a reduction in costs resulting in increase profits.

- Quality of service will increase, and it will be possible to rationalise service schedules.

- The establishment of new techniques that would greatly improve the service.

- There will be rationalisation of contracts between the company and its sub-contractors.

- The relationships between departments will improve.

- More up-to-date reports and data will be provided.

- Communication will improve and will flow more freely within the company.

- Good communication systems will ensure that all communications are; clear, easy to read and understand and consistent in style, format and corporate image.

- E-communications readiness will be developed across all departments.

- There will be effective use of technology to support internal and external communications.

- The company will have procedures in place to deal with situations where relationships breakdown.

- Equipment and facilities will be installed and repaired more rationally.

- There should also be an improvement in human relationships.

This, I am confident, will result in; continuous improvement and increase in the company's share of the market create consistency of purpose to continually improve the service. The company will cease its dependency or need for inspection on a mass basis, break down of barriers between departments and barriers that rob employees of their pride of workmanship will be removed.

Nottingham City Council (Ncc) Expepience

Nottingham City Council and Democracy

Nottingham City Council is an all-purpose unitary authority, providing all local government services within the City of Nottingham administrative district and working with other organisations to make Nottingham a better place in which to live, work, visit and invest. Like all local authorities, the

Council is a democratic organisation, with 55 councillors representing electors in the 20 electoral wards in the City of Nottingham. There is a local election every four years when all 55 seats are contested.

The councillors meet, as a full council, around every six weeks. A limited number of items of business are taken during those meetings, such as, approving the level of council expenditure. The full council must consider council tax. However, the council delegates authority for making its main decisions in several ways.

Best Value Performance Plan

The City Council is required to, publish a "Best Value Performance Plan", by the end of June every year. The "Plan" sets out the City Council's vision, ambition and priorities for the forthcoming years, and a review of performance in the last financial year. In the review of performance, detailed information is presented in the form of "Best Value Performance Indicators", which all Councils have to publish and which allow comparisons to be made. The forward planning is presented in the "Corporate Plan (2006-11)" for the Council, which aligns to the recently launched "Partnership Plan" for Nottingham, "One Nottingham-One Plan".

Central Government has recently revised their guidance for the production of the "Performance Plan". An example is the Nottingham City Council's Performance Plan, which is made up of the "Corporate Plan (2006-11)".

Nottingham's Constitution

The Constitution is part of the Council's corporate governance framework, which defines the systems and processes by which the council; leads, directs and controls its functions and relates to its communities and partners. The purpose of the Constitution is, to set out how the Council; conducts its business, how decisions are made and the procedures that are followed to ensure that these decisions are effective, efficient and transparent, so that the Council remains accountable to local people. Some of these procedures are required by law, while others are a matter for the Council to determine. The Council will exercise all its powers and duties, in accordance with the law and its approved constitution.

Nottingham City Council's constitution, which is divided into ten parts, was updated in 2005 and took effect from 18 July 2005.

The Core Constitution and the Constitution appendices.

The Constitution of Nottingham City Council, under the Local Government Act 2000 and associated directions, sets out the basic rules governing the Council's business.

Council Responsibilities

Most of us plan for emergencies. We may; give spare keys to neighbours, carry a donor card or first aid kit, even if we don't expect a problem. Local Authorities also plan for the worst, but on a larger scale. Emergency planning involves; assessing risks and where possible mitigating them, tackling major emergencies, carrying on business as usual and restoring normality afterwards.

The emergency services, local authorities, businesses, voluntary groups and many other bodies, all produce plans, to deal with any form of major incident. They are all based on the concept of "Integrated Emergency Management". Plans should be flexible and focused on the response to an incident rather than its cause. Arrangements should be built into the organisation's everyday working structure. The activities of different departments should be integrated, and arrangements should be co-ordinated with those of other agencies. The common objectives of an integrated response are to:

- Save life

- Prevent escalation

- Relieve suffering

- Safeguard the environment

- Protect property

- Facilitate investigation and enquiries

- Inform the public

- Promote self-help and recovery

- Restore normality as soon as possible.

Nottingham City Council has been actively planning and preparing, as detailed above, for many years.

Nottingham's Area Committees

What they do & how they work

They approve, ensure the delivery of and monitor neighbourhood action plans and other relevant area plans.

They lead and co-ordinate regeneration and renewal activity at an area level.

They undertake and co-ordinate consultation within their areas.

Within budgetary limits, they are empowered to undertake any measures, to achieve the following objectives:

- The promotion or improvement of the economic well being of their area.

- The promotion or improvement of the social well being of their area.

- The promotion or improvement of the environmental well being of their area.

They agree priorities, work programmes and variations in performance standards, including the Neighbourhood Renewal processes, in respect of the following services:

- Footpaths replacement

- Street lighting

- Patch maintenance

- Grounds maintenance, on community parks and playgrounds - excluding heritage sites -.

In respect of services in the local area, and if urgent, via a panel of the Chair, Vice-Chair, an opposition member - if there is one - and a community representative, to approve:

- Housing environmental improvements

- Highway environmental improvements of a local nature

- Minor traffic schemes, diversions and closures under Highways and road traffic legislation, of a local nature.

- Applications for footpath closures, on grounds of amenity or development and to be consulted on proposals for the following services, in relation to the local area:-

  Licensing applications
  Strategic planning applications

  Schools re-organisation

- Detailed proposals for landscaping, open space provision, park equipment provision and other local enhancements relating to agreements under section 106 of the Town and Country Planning Act 1990 and section 278 of the Highways Act 1980.

They are part of the process for monitoring and scrutinising, the performance of local services - provided by the Council and other bodies - and provide feedback and recommendations on their effectiveness, to the Executive Board and the Advice and Scrutiny Committee, to include:

- Refuse collection

- Housing - void properties

- Community Safety

- Voluntary sector grants – a half yearly report

They contribute to the Council's "Best Value Reviews".

They advise the Executive Board, and Advice and Scrutiny Committee, on local needs and priorities and on the impact of Council policy on their areas.

They input local needs and priorities, identified through area working, to the preparation of corporate budgets, policies and strategies.

They prepare, implement and review local projects in consultation with local communities and secure funding from appropriate sources.

They build partnerships between other; public, private, voluntary and community organisations, local residents' and tenants' associations.

They suggest and/or approve proposals of local significance, to rationalise the City Council's operational property holdings and to be consulted, on any proposals to dispose of operational property holdings. In their area of more than local significance, they are responsible for; the proportion of capital receipts to be retained, in accordance with a scheme to be determined by the Executive Board.

They allocate grants in amounts not exceeding £5000 to community or voluntary organisations, for purposes of benefit to the area covered by the committee, within a framework to be approved and reviewed, from time to time, by the Executive Board.

They make appointments to outside bodies - where the body relates to the area concerned - as specified by the Executive Board.

They approve any further matters delegated, from time to time, by Council or the Executive Board.

Partnerships

This project is a network of a number of cities, led by Liverpool and with Nottingham as a partner.

The private sector is increasingly involved in regenerating cities, and in particular those run down areas that are most severely deprived / excluded. The role of the private sector is two fold; firstly to bring resource - both expertise & funding - and secondly to drive and coordinate the regeneration initiatives, attract investors and generate market confidence.

Experience shows that, achieving a better social mix and more functional diversity in cities, and especially in the most deprived areas, are fundamental preconditions for a successful urban regeneration, based on the assessment that, a balanced urban development, can only be achieved if every part of the city can sustain a property market. In this perspective, the role of small pioneer investors appears to be crucial, and the first comers play an important role in "prime pumping" urban regeneration. This is often the case of local companies and/or professionals for economic activities, and pioneer groups or individuals, for the housing market. How to attract those investments is a very important issue for urban regeneration, since it can show community or citizens, are confident in the future success of regeneration initiatives.

Urban cities, have been at the forefront of pioneering new ways of forming partnerships with the private sector, to bring about urban renewal and this project drew out best practice that can be of benefit to others, and some recommendations on policy and legislation implications that may help inform future decisions - EU, national, local - in this field.

Living in Nottingham

The City of Nottingham, lies at the heart of the largest and most populated area in the East Midlands, but only 40% of people in the urban area – which is one of the most populated in England - live within the Nottingham City's boundary. The influence of Nottingham extends beyond its boundaries with regards to leisure, culture and employment. The retail catchments extend even further to include Derbyshire, Lincolnshire and Leicestershire. Most of the people living outside the city boundary, reside in the more affluent suburbs, whilst those living within the city limits, experience disproportionate levels of depravation. However, the characteristic of Nottingham City, as a whole, when assessed for education, health and depravation are in line with the national averages and, Nottingham is like many other cities.

Nottingham City Council's objective is – according to one senior councillor – to improve the standard of living for the people of Nottingham. To achieve this we must increase the skill levels and educational attainment of those living in the most deprived wards, so that they have a route to economic security and enable them to share in the success of the city. To achieve this, we have to change the culture of low expectation, low self esteem and dependency. He said:

> "This is why increasing the number of adults who are active economically and raising the levels of attainment in education amongst our young people, form part of our highest priorities."

Another senior councillor said:

> "Nottingham City Council is committed to providing the community leadership that will create sustainable, cohesive and vibrant communities with a good mix of public and private housing, income and ethnicity. Over the next few years, we aim to make significant improvements in the quality of life of the people in the City of Nottingham who experience discrimination and disadvantage, by challenging the culture of dependency and low expectation, and will tackle social exclusion and the lack of cohesion between different communities."

Nottingham City Council (NCC) Approach to TQM

Restructure

In order to improve the quality and effectiveness of its services, NCC under-took a TQM approach to service delivery.

NCC restructured all its departments to better reflect the generic grouping of Direct, Corporate and Central Support Services. One consequence of this restructure has been the removal of two departments. NCC decided that the process of regrouping services would reduce or remove organisational barriers to quick and effective action.

It was felt and accepted by most managers within NCC and elected members, that the existing management hierarchies did not work in the best interest of the people of Nottingham and was not best value for money. Therefore, one important objective of restructuring has been the creation of flatter management structures for departments. The removal of tiers of management at various levels and the standardisation of job descriptions, lead to the creation of clearer lines of responsibilities and accountability for the delivery of the Council's services.

Chief and Assistant Chief Officers, have, as a consequence of reorganisation / restructuring, been ascribed a much more strategic management role with greater emphasis on forward planning and responding to NCC's corporate objectives, and less on the day-to-day involvement with operational matters.

R. Ashley Rawlins TD. DL.

The Old Organisation Structure

The original organisation structure was similar to what Henry Mintzberg called "The Machine Organisation" structure [3]. This structure he argued is the offspring of the industrial revolution, when jobs became highly specialised and work became highly standardised. However, this structure resulted in a large number of middle managers, who controlled the highly specialised work of the operating core.

The middle line hierarchy was structured on a functional basis, all the way to the top, where the real power of coordination – with a centralised administration core – lies. So this structure was rather centralised and this enabled the top managers to maintain central control over the organisation.

The Machine Organisation Structure

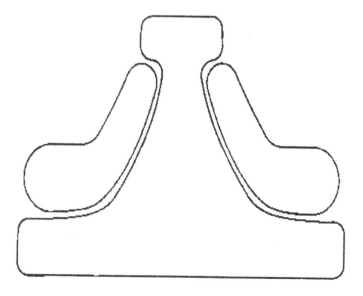

The New Organisation Structure

The intension of the Chief Executive Officer – Professor Ted Cantel – was, to change the organisation's structure to a structure that would give more autonomy to departments.

The idea put forward, was an organisation with a flatter structure, similar to what Mintzberg caller "The Professional Organisation" structure.

This structure was chosen because, as Mintzberg argued [4], although it has a bureaucratic configuration, it relies on the standardisation of skills, for its coordination, and unlike "The Machine Organisation" structure, the professionals dominate the organisation. However, one draw-back with this type of structure is that the organisation relies heavily on trained professionals – people highly specialised and with considerable control over their own work – resulting in, the organisation surrendering a lot of its power, not only to the professionals, but also to the institutions and associations that selects and train them.

Mintzberg argues that this structure requires the organisation to be highly decentralised horizontally; with power over many decisions, strategic and operational, flowing all the way down the hierarchy, to the professional of the operating core. This is exactly what professor Ted Cantel hoped to achieve through the NCC's TQM programme.

The Professional Organisation Structure

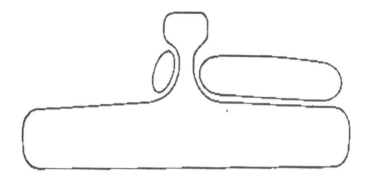

The New Structure – Modified

During the planning stage of the TQM programme, the organisation's top managers realised that, if departments were to achieve the level of autonomy, at the level required for the proper implementation of the TQM programme, a modification of the suggested new structure was required.

After several "discussion group meetings", of senior managers and a number of seminars with senior and middle managers, a modified organisation structure was developed, which looked similar to what Mintzberg called "The Diversified Organisation Structure" [5].

Because each department, provide a specific service to the people of Nottingham and to other NCC's departments, it was necessary – for quality and efficiency of service provision – that the central administration be decentralised, so that senior managers could have direct control and managerial responsibilities, over the administration services that are supporting their departments.

The Diversified Organisation Structure

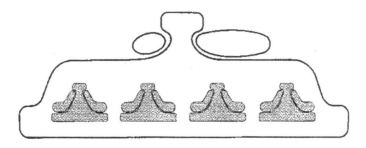

Mintzberg argues [5] that this structure is suitable for organisations, whose products or services are diversified on product/service lines – much like NCC – and grant considerable autonomy to each unit/department to run its own business. This he argued result in a form of decentralisation, down the chain of command.

Central headquarters, maintain a semblance of control over the departments by the use of direction supervision. However, too much of that will interfere with the departments' autonomy. Mintzberg suggests [5] that headquarters departments should rely on performance control systems and the standardisation of outputs to achieve this control. NCC achieved this control by requiring each department, to bid for the funds necessary for the efficient delivery of the department's services through; service level agreements, service plans and business plans. These are reviewed on an annual basis.

Reporting directly to Assistant and Chief Officers, Service Managers have been appointed, with clear responsibilities for all operational matters within each of NCC's 127 service areas.

Each service team is required to produce a Service Plan, setting out how the service is to be developed and managed. Through the Service Plans, objectives and targets are set for each service. As well as being service specific, these objectives must respond to NCC's core values and the manifesto of the current political administration. Moreover, each Service Plan is based on a cost centre and identifies performance indicators, through which, progress and achievements can be monitored.

A clear set of management responsibilities have been devolved to Service Managers, enabling them to manage and develop the services in a much better and more efficient way, in response to customers' or clients' needs. These responsibilities include; personnel, training, market research, team building, equality and customer care. Financial regulations have also been changed, gradually over a period of time, to allow Service Managers greater flexibility.

Direct and immediate access to support is available, through the devolution of central support staff, to "Support Service Teams" located within departments. Such teams, led by a Support Services Manager, includes; Personnel Officers, Finance Staff, Business Analysts, Training and Equality Officers.

Within this culture, performance indicators are critical. Generally, only cost information of the most basic type has been available. The emphasis now is placed on qualitative and quantitative measures, together with the recognition that user/customer satisfaction must be the principal measure of service effectiveness. In addition to the performance indicators, a range of key indicators are identified by which overall departmental performance can be monitored and regularly reported to Member Committees. It was envisaged that this process would also go a long way in assisting NCC to respond better, to the Government's Citizens' Charter, which requires local authority organisations to collect and publish performance information.

Quality Systems

Quality Assurance Managers have been appointed in both of NCC's Contracts Departments –Nottingham City Contracts Works (NCCW) and Nottingham City Building Works (NCBW) – where BS 5750 accreditation has been achieved for a range of services. The managers of these departments introduced their quality systems because; they wanted to be one step ahead of the government, who at that time was working on proposals, to impose CCT on all local authority organisations. These departments were therefore, in a good position to play a leading role in the NCC's TQM programme.

In addition, all departments now have the service of a dedicated Business Analyst, part of whose remit is to assist Service Managers with the development of their quality systems.

"Team Briefings" have been introduced, for all employees, on a regular basis and is the principal mechanism for a two-way flow of information between senior managers and front-line staff. To facilitate this process, a "Management Briefing" newsletter is being circulated on a regular basis, giving details of new policies and procedures for discussion at team briefings.

A "Staff Survey" was carried out, to establish the views and attitudes of employees to such issues as:

1. Job satisfaction.

2. Employee information.

3. Stress.

4. Training provision.

5. Career development.

6. Equality of opportunity.

7. Supervisors' performance.

8. Communication between teams and between departments.

The survey provided a wealth of information, which was then used to inform and develop NCC's human resources strategy. It is expected that this exercise will be repeated on a regular basis to; monitor trends, contribute to and assess the impact of change.

Around 350 managers have taken part in a management development programme, which was intended to provide a foundation in; setting and achieving objectives, identifying and responding to customer needs, marketing, improving accessibility, etc. This programme will continue in the current and future years, using NCC's in-house team of consultants, to develop the necessary training, linked to; performance management, staff review and appraisal, team building and the development of a more participative management style.

Councillors – Elected Members – are also Strategic Managers, and they will need to be kept abreast of key issues that are affecting local government in general and NCC in particular. An introductory programme, for new Councillors, was successfully completed in 1993. A series of wide-ranging seminars have also taken place during 1994 and 1995. Such seminars were expected to take place in future years and I understand that that is the case, although they are not taking place every year, as previously expected.

Staff Reaction to the Programme

NCC's Director of Social Services said:

> "If you ask people for their definition of quality of service you will get many different answers, and the same goes for TQM. Although we are not going for BS 5750, we have included some aspects of it in our TQM approach to service delivery, for example; we have a small quality assurance team. They provide an enabling role, and do not act as quality police. That is not their remit. TQM does not belong to top management, it is the responsibility of all managers, but we have aimed it at everyone in the organisation. We want everyone in the organisation to claim ownership of this TQM thing, and take responsibility for the quality of every thing they do. Quality for us is customer driven so, we organise customer surveys to identify where we are failing the customer and then take positive actions to rectify those problems. I must say that in some cases we are unable to satisfy

the customers' needs completely, because of limited resources. We are getting less and less resources to do more and more, but we never leave the customer in limbo. We always explain to our customers what is possible and what is not possible."

NCBW Quality Manager said:

"We had to read a lot and we had to learn fast, but it still took us 18 months to set up and test our quality systems. We employed consultants as advisers. They were helpful but very expensive because, they charged on a day rate basis per visit but they did not give us any information unless we asked for it. What made it so expensive, was the fact that we did not know what we required so, we did not know what questions to ask, and if we did not ask the question, we did not get the information. As soon as we were able to struggle through on our own we stopped using the consultants and did not invite back.

You must have the full support of all your staff, this is most important. Without the support of all staff – including senior managers – we would have failed. We sold it to staff as "their system", it is owned by each section and each individual so, everyone gave it full commitment because no one wants it to be said that he or she let the side down."

NCBW Assistant Quality Manager said:

"We have a system in place, we have published the procedures and everyone is doing their best to make it work, but there are still problems. People are expected to look at the way they do things and to come up with ideas to modify the procedures, but some people are not reporting the modifications and this is just as costly, if not more costly, than keeping the old procedures. We overcame this problem by employing Quality Auditors – through training of some existing staff and internal promotions – to undertake quality audits.

The training for these Auditors' positions was very expensive because, it meant training a lot of people. The Quality Auditors go into other sections in their departments and carry out quality audits on that section; we then use the information from the audit to update the operations procedures centrally. A Quality Auditor is not allowed to audit his own section. We have two people in each section who are quality audit trained.

We are quite happy with the systems now, but it was not easy. We had to put a lot of work into it, but now we have operations procedures for each section, both in folders and on computer. Having the procedures on computer is good for us because, some sections have overlapping procedures so, if one section change one of its procedures, the computer will identify all sections with a similar procedure and update their operating procedures. Just in case people go for some time without checking for procedural changes on their computer, a paper memo is sent automatically, to all sections that are affected by the changes."

One Quality Auditor said:

"We are coping well with all the changes and managing the operations is so much simpler now because, everyone feel that they have a responsibility, not just to making the systems work, but to look for ways of improving the systems and assist with the implementation of those improvements. However, this also caused some problems because; people became so enthusiastic about implementing improvements that some improvements are implemented without the necessary communication and feedback. This is where the Quality Auditors come into their own, as they are able to pick up these changes and ensure that they are fed back to the centre and communicated to everyone who will be affected."

One Senior Engineer said:

"I have been employed by Nottingham City Council for over 25 years and these changes, which includes the implementation of a TQM programme is one of our best achievements in a very long time. As professionals, we have always managed ourselves, in that we take full responsibility for the decisions that we make, but having our own dedicated support staff, make my department and sections much more efficient. I come to work now feeling a lot better than I have done for a number of years, knowing that I do not have to spend most of my working day fighting with central admin to get simple things done, for example; specifications prepared on time, tender documents prepared accurately and on time, correspondence between NCC's professional staff and clients / contractors meet specified timescales, etc.

Our appraisal system, I think is good. Most organisations link their appraisal system to pay, as a way of getting more work out of people, but that is not the case with NCC. We use our appraisal system as a way of developing our staff to their best potential. It is not cheap so we have to include staff development costs in our; service plans, business plans and action plans and this comes out in our annual budget requirements.

Staff development training usually takes place in-house – although not usually on site – and senior managers take a keen interest and sometimes attend these courses themselves. The Chief Executive – Professor Ted Cantel – has also attend some of these training sessions and took part in workshops associated with those training sessions.

I think that we are benefiting from the changes that we made and especially the TQM programme implementation. Staffs are working better, there is more team work, there have been reduction in staff absence through illness, projects costs have been reduced because we are able to build better working relationships between NCC's professionals and contractors and have much better communication between; ourselves, contractors, other departments and our clients."

One Senior Architect said:

"The department has become very flexible in its approach to work, so people move around the department and help each other. You do not get a situation where one architect is struggling to meet a deadline and another architect is taking things easy. No! The architect with little work will rally round and help the other architect to meet his / her deadline. The engineers are the same, they would not sit around whilst others are struggling, they help each other out and departments are benefiting from this collaborative style of working. People were not trained to work in this collaborative way, it just evolved out of the TQM programme and the new work ethos that is customer driven.

The changes we made, together with the implementation of the TQM programme, have made departments more efficient and managing staff is a lot easier now, because people are taking more responsibility for the work that they do and the service they provide. I believe that we have the right things and a good balance have been struck. It is not easy to change people, it is not something that can be done overnight and changing an organisation's culture through training does not always work, but in our case it did work and is still working because people were interested in the work they did. Yes! I feel that we got the balance right between the change in organisation culture and job satisfaction.

People require satisfaction from their jobs, if they are to feel any sense of achievement. People will not be committed to the organisation and its objectives if they get no satisfaction from the work that they do. In my department, everyone gets satisfaction from the work they do. I know that they do from staff and customer surveys and from staff appraisals. TQM requires everyone to work together and people in my department are doing just that. I believe that people will only work together if they have job satisfaction and are committed to quality improvement."

A second Service Manager with 15 years service said:

"The Staff Appraisal system, from NCC's point of view, is good because it is about staff development and improving the efficiency and effectiveness of our work and the services that we provide to the community. I understand that some local authorities link their staff appraisal to some kind of performance related pay. I have never worked for one of those authorities, but I feel that linking staff appraisal to performance related pay is bad for those organisations. With such systems, people will be competing with each other rather than working together to make their organisation more efficient. Managing professional people is in itself a complicated task; therefore, managing a professional organisation where professional people are continually competing against each other must be like managing an organisation that is in continuous crisis. I am pleased that we did not go down that route.

Our staff appraisal system is about developing our people, so that they could achieve their full potential. If we as managers can achieve this, we will have people who are; committed to the objective that we agreed, feel that they are getting more job satisfaction, better motivated to satisfy customers' / clients' needs and committed to quality improvements. If we have people who are; working together for the benefit of our customers, willing to monitor their work, are completely satisfy with the services they provide and totally committed to quality improvement then we are well on the way to meeting the requirements of the TQM programme. I feel safe in saying that we are doing all that and more."

A third Service Manager said:

"Through the TQM programme, we are encouraging all our people to provide a standard of work that is second to none. As a local authority organisation, I feel that the customer services we provide are amongst the best in the UK. The key to this success is due mainly to the large number of great leaders – identified through the TQM programme -, making the most of all the talents that we have in the organisation and exploring organisational opportunities – internal and external -. We want all of our people to be company people, driven by continuous quality improvement and achieving that is the focus of our people strategy.

We are aware of our responsibilities to our customers/clients – reinforced through various training packages – and are committed to customer satisfaction. We are determined that our good reputation – as seen by our customers and other local authorities – will continue. We have commissioned surveys of; our employees, our customers/clients and other organisations that are providing similar services. This allows us to; benchmark our performance, as an organisation, against similar organisations, identify and share best practice and focus our efforts on the issues that mean most to our customers and employees.

Through the various training packages that we have developed - which is part of the TQM programme -, we were able to deal adequately with the challenges thrown up by the rapid external and internal environmental changes faced by local authority organisations. This we achieved by; building very good leadership across the whole organisation, managing in a way that encourages and enable all our people to achieve their potential and the devolution of power for decision-making to departments and service areas.

The complete restructure of the organisation – again, part of the TQM programme – brought about rapid improvements in both efficiency and the services that we provide to our customers. We are able to evidence these improvements through the; staff reviews, employee surveys and customer surveys.

We value diversity, and respect for others, in the workplace, is a fundamental part of our organisational culture. Through the TQM programme, we have introduced a range of recruitment practices, aimed at attracting people from varying backgrounds and different groupings. We have developed and provided tools to encourage our employees to engage with and understand NCC's diversity agenda."

A fourth Service Manager said:

"We had a general awareness of quality control systems because; prior to the introduction of the TQM programme, a number of our departments had installed quality control systems - in readiness for the government's imposed CCT – and achieved BS5750 certification, the British Standards quality mark. The quality control systems were installed to make those departments more efficient and as competitive as private organisations, that were providing similar services, and who will be competing with local authority departments under the imposed CCT.

It was the intention of NCC that all departments would seek BS5750 certification, but this was something for the future. Rapid changes were taking place in our internal and external environment and to cope with these rapid changes, the organisation had to develop new strategies to meet the changing demands. This required all of us as NCC's employees to change the organisation's culture, through the way we; work, communicate and interact with each other and our customers/clients.

Since the BS accreditation was not going to be made compulsory for other departments and there was the necessity to restructure the whole organisation to make it more efficient and customer driven, it was decided that we would not seek BS accreditation for other departments, but restructure the whole organisation and introduce the TQM programme. These changes involved everyone in the organisation, including the Chief Executive. We are continuing to make progress as an organisation. It is important that we don't see TQM as simply a slogan; it has to be fundamental to the way we operate and provide services. Through the TQM programme, we are able to position ourselves to take advantage of future opportunities, anticipate our customers' aspirations and develop strategies that lead to exceptional performance and customer services amongst all our employees."

NCC's Director of Design & Property Services said:

"It was our intention to seek to try and improve the services that we provide, by developing quality systems that would enable us to achieve BS5750 accreditation. However, this was not something that we were going to do in the short term because; we were not subject to the government's CCT. It was not imposed on us.

After the decision was taken to restructure the organisation and introduce a TQM programme, we – the senior managers – felt that BS5750 accreditation was not necessary because the TQM programme covered what we would have achieved through BS5750 and a lot more. In discussions with the departments that had achieved BS5750 accreditation – because of necessity – they said that the only benefit they derived from BS5750 is that when they compete with private organisations BS5750 is usually one of the requirements. On the other-hand it is very expensive and time consuming.

The time, expense and effort that were required to achieve BS5750 were put into the introduction of the TQM programme. The departments that had achieved BS5750 accreditation, were not exempt the changes that were taking place within NCC. They were part of the restructuring – and rightly so – including the introduction of the TQM programme. They, like us, had to carry out staff surveys to establish the views and attitudes of employees to issues such as; job satisfaction, employee information / communication, stress, training provision, career development, equality of opportunity and the performance of managers and team leaders.

All managers and most trainee managers were required to take part in management development programmes aimed at providing a good foundation in; setting and achieving objectives, identifying and responding to customer needs / demands, marketing, improving accessibility and improving communication both internally and externally. This programme is on-going and to facilitate this, we are using an in-house team of consultants to develop training packages that are linked to; performance management, staff review and appraisal, developing management styles that are more proactive, and team building exercises. We wanted to develop an organisation that was more; efficient in the way we did our business, accountable in the way we spends the public's money, responsive to our customers' and clients' requirements.

To achieve this, a change of organisation culture was necessary. Installing quality control systems - BS5750 or any other BS – by themselves would not have enabled us to achieve the culture change that was required for the organisation. By restructuring the organisation and introducing TQM we have achieved that change in our approach to; our work, the way we communicate with each other, the way we communicate with people outside the organisation, accountability, setting and meeting demanding targets and customer and client satisfaction. Those people who found it too difficult to adapt to the new organisation culture have resigned and found other jobs or have taken early retirement. That was a little unfortunate because, we lost some people with a lot of public sector experience, never-the-less, it gave us the opportunity to recruit people who were enthusiastic in the new organisational culture that we wanted to achieve.

All these changes – organisation restructure and TQM – were designed to restore client / customer confidence in the services that we provide and we have seen the following:

- An increase in the company's ability to meet customers' and clients' expectations.

- We get this information from the regular surveys that we undertake.

- An increase in staff expertise through organised staff development and training. We get this information from; staff surveys, staff annual reviews and appraisals.

- The ability to maintain good and effective relationships with; our service users, other organisations and between departments.

- The ability to assess whether customers are getting value for money when we provide services. We achieve this through benchmarking.

  Attention is also paid to the ethical use of services and performance as well as the adoption of corporate standards.

> Our people are working particularly hard
> in responding to the unusually demanding
> environment brought about by the change in
> organisation culture. As Senior Managers,
> we have to thank all our employees for their
> loyalty, commitment and dedication."

From my discussions with; senior managers, other employees, clients and end users of Nottingham City Council's services, it seems to me that in pursuing a change in organisation culture through the introduction of a TQM programme, NCC have addressed what the Author of this book termed in a previous writing –The Millennium Manager - "The Importance of Quality".

Within an organisation, according to R. Ashley Rawlins [6]; management, employees, materials, facilities, processes, and equipment all affect quality. The manager must be able to identify these aspects, and seek to understand how they interact in the organisation. Once a strategy is developed and communicated and the key variables affecting quality are understood, the conversion function can take place. Services are generated. Customers are satisfied. Some popular concepts of quality are:

1. Quality is fitness for use.

2. Quality is doing it right the first time and every time.

3. Quality is the customer's perception.

4. Quality provides a product or service at a price that the customer can afford.

The key then, is the awareness of the need to improve, and then to select improvement techniques with the best chance of success. An operating philosophy is required to establish and maintain an environment, which will result in never ending improvement in the quality and productivity of products and services throughout the organisation, its supply base, and its dealer organisations.

This I argued requires the organisation to improve quality and productivity of every element of the business from planning to field service. It includes; all products and services, people relationships, attention to customers' needs, shareholders' investments, and management approaches. Finally, it must be "customer driven".

British Telecom (BT) Experience

About British Telecom

BT consists mainly of four Business lines:

1. BT Global Services.

2. BT Openreach.

3. BT Retail.

4. BT Wholesale.

BT Openreach was established early 2006 in response to Ofcom's strategic review of the telecommunications industry. It operates the physical – as opposed to the electronic – assets of the local access networks and provides the services that use these networks to communications providers, both internally and externally.

BT Openreach, BT Retail and BT Wholesale operate within the UK, where BT – from its market share - is said to be the UK's largest communications service provider. BT supplies the residential and business sectors with a wide range of communications products and services. It also offers a comprehensive range of managed and packaged communications solutions.

BT Global services addresses the networked IT services needs of multi-site organisations both in the UK and internationally.

BT Retail – from its market share - is said to be the UK's largest communications service provider to the residential and business sectors. It trades under one of the UK's leading brands – BT – and is the main channel to market in the UK for other businesses in the BT Group. It supplies a wide range of communications products and services, including; voice, data, internet and multimedia services, and offers a comprehensive range of managed and packaged communications solutions. Its portfolio includes; telephone products such as calls, analogue/digital lines and private circuits. Recently, it has been focusing on; broadband, mobility and networked IT services.

BT Wholesale provides network services and solutions within the UK. Its customers include; communications companies, fixed and mobile network operators, internet and other service providers. The customer base also includes BT Retail and BT Global services. Most of BT Wholesale's revenue is internal and mainly represents trading with BT Retail.

BT Global Services supplies managed services and solutions to multi-site organisations worldwide. Its target market is multi-site organisations including large companies with significant global requirements, together with large companies trading in local markets. It provides them with networked IT services and a complete range of managed solutions.

Innovation

Through innovation BT is able to identify innovations in; products, services and technologies globally, bringing them together with the work of the people at BT. This helps to ensure that there is no gap between what is possible and what is delivered into the markets being served by BT.

Open innovation takes BT beyond its own people to work with; partners, customers, suppliers and universities in what it calls innovation networks. According to Ben Verwaayen – BT's Chief Executive:

> "For us, innovation is about being open and collaborative – working together to turn good ideas into great innovations that help make people's lives simpler and more enjoyable. Innovation applies to all parts of our business – from the way we come up with, develop and sell our services to the way we organise our operations."

British Telecom's Approach to TQM

British Telecom's approach to TQM was similar to BA's approach. BT's TQM programme was launched in 1984. Management Consultants were imported from America to train all of BT's managers over a six months period. Managers were expected – after their training – to train all of their employees over a three months period. However, not all employees received the training but senior managers assumed that the necessary training had taken place and the TQM programme was implemented.

This apparent lack of training and initial preparation, to get all its people on board the TQM train before the programme was implemented, meant that the organisation was not "people ready", There were no commitment to the TQM programme – not even amongst its managers – and any attempt at changing the organisation's culture – in that type of environment - was doomed from the start. According to one retired BT Engineer who was a level-2 manager during the TQM programme implementation:

> "The organisation was not ready for a TQM programme. That required a change to how people approached their work and the time was not right for that. There were too many things happening at the time that managers and their staff had to deal with; rapid changes in communications technology requiring a lot of training for staff, reduction in staffing levels and the relocation of some staff because fewer buildings and maintenance engineers were required, and industrial actions by the trade unions.
>
> We were not ready for TQM and I do not believe that the consultants did the job they were paid to do. I understand that they were paid hundreds of thousands of pounds, yet as a level-2 manager I did not meet with any of them. I received no training from

the consultants in respect of the TQM programme; neither did any of my level-1 managers. I received 8 completed ring-binders with the title "British Telecom – Total Quality Management" and these were to be distributed to my level-1 managers and one for myself. They looked impressive but as a total quality tool, they meant nothing.

A number of my level-1 managers – who had formal management qualifications in addition to their engineering qualifications – were promoted to level-2 managers and moved to a central office to form what they called "Quality Teams". I never understood what they did and they were never able to explain to me what they did, except to say, that there work entail giving advice on quality systems.

My understanding of TQM was that the training – necessary to bring about culture change within the organisation – and the quality systems should be in place before the TQM programme was implemented, but that did not happen in our case. BT thought it best to throw a lot of money at it and assumed that that was what was required. The hard work and total commitment from the top all the way down the organisation was ignored. However, during the 1980s and 1990s, TQM was the craze – especially in large organisations – and is still the craze in today's business and manufacturing industries, with service and third sector

R. Ashley Rawlins TD. DL.

> organisations joining the band-wagon. With
> this type of attitude in large organisations,
> TQM is bound to Fail."

This retired BT manager seems to be suggesting that BT's TQM programme had failed due to; lack of appropriate training, lack of commitment from senior managers, poor timing, poor communication, and the organisation culture change necessary for successful TQM implementation had not taken place. The organisation did not undertake the necessary preparation before attempting the implementation of TQM and was not ready.

TQM Programme Implementation

The task of implementing TQM can be daunting for the senior management team, because different organisations require different approach when preparing themselves for the implementation of a TQM programme. The first decision is where to start and this can be so difficult that many organisations make several mistakes, on the way, and others never get started.

The preliminary stages of understanding and commitment are vital first steps, which also form the foundation of the whole TQM structure. Some organisations skip these phases – at their peril -, believing that they have the right attitude, culture and awareness, when in fact there are some fundamental gaps in their quality creditability. These will soon lead to insurmountable difficulties and sometimes failure.

While an intellectual understanding of quality provides a basis for TQM, it is clearly only the start of the TQM process. The understanding must be translated into; commitment, policies, plans and action for TQM to be communicated to all employees and be accepted – at least in principle -. Making this happen requires not only commitment, but also a competence in the mechanics of quality management, and in making and managing changes. Without a strategy to implement TQM through systems, capability and control, the expended effort – in time and money - will lead to frustration or failure.

The implementation begins with the drawing up of a quality policy statement, and the establishment of the appropriate organisational structure, both for managing and encouraging quality through teamwork. Collecting information on how the organisation operates, including the cost of quality, helps to identify the main areas where organisational culture change is required and in which improvement will have the largest impact on performance. Planning improvement involves all managers, but a critical early stage involves, putting quality management systems in place – if they do not already exist - to drive the improvement process and make sure that problems remain solved, using structured corrective action procedures.

Once the plans and quality systems have been put into place, the need for continued education, training and communication becomes paramount – a process that does not appear in BT's TQM implementation procedures -.

Organisations that try to change their; quality culture, management systems, procedures, and/or control methods without effective two-way communications, will experience staff frustration of being left out of the decision making process, employees will not be committed to the development and success – long term or otherwise -. Such organisations may continue to function but will be unable inspire confidence – amongst its employees and customers- in being able to survive the changing market environment in which it operates. Such lack of confidence cost BT dearly – in financial terms – as its share price fell from £12 in the late 1990s to £1.50 in the early 2000s.

Organisations with a good understanding of quality and how it should be managed would experience the following:

- There will be top management commitment.

- There will be written quality policies.

- There will be a satisfactory organisational structure.

- It is ready to begin the planning stage.

When implementation of the TQM programme is completed, priorities amongst the various departments and projects must be identified. For example; a quality system, which conforms to the requirements of ISO 9000 or BS 5750 series may be helpful – if they already exists -, but systems for quality will not be a major task for the organisation, however, introducing a quality-related costing system may well be a major task for any organisation introducing a TQM programme. A review of the company's current performance in all the areas of its operations - even those that are well established -, should be part of normal operations to ensure continuous improvement.

BT's Reputation

According to a Senior Manager in BT's Leeds Area and a Board Member:

"Our success depends on responding to changes in our market environment – including consumer tastes – by nurturing existing excellent communication systems and creating new ones. We have been through many changes but we have always worked together to create new systems that helps people to improve their communication, both at home and at work.

Our reputation is of crucial importance to the Company and everyone who works in it. Every employee in the Company – individually and collectively – has the role of guarding our reputation and I know they share with me a commitment to ensure that we do not let our customers and ourselves down.

Our reputation is fundamental to our continued success over many years. We continue to build on our long tradition of corporate and social responsibility, ensuring that our commitment and policies remain true to our heritage in an ever changing environment. Good corporate and social responsibility encompass areas such as; customer needs, responsible marketing, sustainable environment, employee engagement and diversity, ethical trading, and corporate governance. We have made significant improvement in all these areas, enabling us to concentrate on developing more innovative initiatives.

Our TQM programme is working well, although some people can't remember it happening. Because of all the redundancies, some members of staff were not happy, however, each BT Region have a team of Quality Managers who are at Senior or Middle Management level, and they are responsible for ensuring that procedural changes are implemented and communicated throughout the organisation. They police the system and they are assets to the organisation. I do not see how we could manage our systems without them."

By the year 2003, British Telecom were failing and saw the price of its shares tumbled from all-time high of over £12.00 each to an all-time low of less than £2.00 each. Some senior managers argued that, BT's problems were the result of poor management decisions at Board level, whilst some employees below managerial level – including some who were made redundant or given early retirement – argued that the demise of BT was not due to fierce competition in the telecom arena, but to junior and middle managers who lacked management skills. Despite the various criticisms – some from present and past employees at managerial levels as recent as early 2007, one Board level manager said:

"BT values capture the way we get things done. They sum up what customers can expect from us and what BT people can expect from each other. They are at the heart of every compelling customer experience. Living our values is key to our success."

Another Board level Director said:

"We aim to create a high-performance team of people who can really make a difference. Ensuring that every single employee has the opportunity to develop innovative solutions and realise his/her potential is the best way we know of meeting and exceeding our customers' expectations.

- We are committed to recruiting, developing, encouraging, and rewarding the best.

- We recognise the power of diversity and are working to create an inclusive working environment in which all employees can thrive.

- We are focused on motivating leaders at all levels in BT and providing appropriate development opportunities."

British Telecom and Workplace Diversity

Many organisations in today's business environment – including BT - are highlighting the growing importance of diversity in the workplace. In some Chinese organisations, their executive boards have placed so much importance on workplace diversity that they have included it as part of their TQM systems.

Diversity in organisations is nothing new. The British Armed Forces have – for many years- used the differences between individuals and styles to enhance team performance. Civilian organisations are beginning to believe that greater understanding, respect and value for the benefits that "difference" can bring are very important issues for the success of organisations in the modern environment, due mainly to a continuous increase in the diverse customer base and labour market, and the introduction of legislations designed to prevent discrimination in the workplace.

BT talks about its responsibility for enabling a diverse workforce as part of its work on inclusion and diversity but it does not seems to me to be linked – in anyway – to the TQM programme, which was implemented in the 1980s. This information does not appear to have filtered down to the rank and file either, because, - having interviewed over 50 engineers and technicians in several Towns and Counties – I have yet to speak with one who has heard of or taken part in BT's "diversity" programme. Never-the-less, one senior board member said:

> "The aim of the programme is to provide a working environment where all employees are equal members of the organisation, from recruitment, into training and beyond. The work undertaken has resulted in adjustments being made to the recruitment process as well as the workplace. Within the recruitment process, consideration is given to issues such as offering support with filling in application forms and providing large font size options for any assessments. Adjustments to the workplace have ranged from redesigning work stations to using clear markings on cupboards and walkways. Buddying arrangements and additional training have also been provided where appropriate. Throughout the process, efforts have been made to discuss issues with employees directly, so that the adjustments

made meet their requirements and allow them to receive the full benefit."

He went on to talk about the "New Electrical Operating Procedure" and linked that operating procedure to BT's inclusion and workplace diversity programmes. He continued:

> "We have introduced a new common operating procedure across electricity distribution that allows employees to isolate – safely – electrical equipment for maintenance. The aim of this change is to ensure employees feel confident they are carrying out their role correctly, regardless of location, and to provide a framework to achieve zero injuries every day. The procedure provides a consistent set of rules and practices, allowing employees to operate across the business. Employees from a wide range of departments came together to develop the processes. In addition to the documentation, a comprehensive training programme was developed and over a period of 5 months, nearly 3000 employees were trained, requiring either a 2 or 3 day course. To meet this intensive programme, more than 90 employees were trained as instructors and at one point, simultaneous training was taking place at 15 different locations."

According to Pam Farmer [7], HR manager for equality and diversity at BT Group; workplace diversity training has taken a foot hold and is providing BT with an expert group of people, throughout the organisation, who are committed and enthusiastic about diversity. She said:

> "The initiative is just part of BT's wide ranging programme on diversity, which encompasses everything from flexible working to procurement. The business also has a number of specialist support groups; a disability network, a women's network, a gay, lesbian and trans-gender network plus others.
>
> The groups meet separately but also regularly get together to discuss common themes. They also have an important input into BT's business development plans. It is a two-way street. The deal is, we are supporting you. What can you do to support us within our communities as well? Groups have advised BT on niche marketing to the Asian community and to gay and lesbian groups. People are committed to BT and they want the company to be healthy and respected in their communities.
>
> BT has found that creative use of internal communication channels has helped to maintain a buzz around diversity. BT's online staff magazine, for example, invites employees to contribute thought pieces on diversity-related issues, and to be frank and open with their views. This has helped to develop a mature, productive debate around some prickly issues.

The organisation's communication has developed to an extent that, we have not come in as a parent and said BT thinks this, but has enabled people to contribute from wherever they are in the organisation. If someone says something we are not comfortable with, we know someone else ah yes, but _____.

There are lots of areas that need to be talked about, but we can't set a policy for all of them and just get every body to do it. The only way it is going to happen is by people talking about these things and owning the issues."

Diversity Legislations

I stated earlier that organisations are beginning to believe that greater understanding, respect and value for the benefits that "difference" can bring are very important issues for the success of organisations in the modern environment, due mainly to a continuous increase in the diverse customer base and labour market, and the introduction of legislations designed to prevent discrimination in the workplace. Therefore, this may be a fitting point to mention something about legislations as they relate to diversity in the workplace.

Diversity is the acceptance of any difference, such as; colour of hair, colour of skin, weight, belief, disability etc. The Home Office has created 6 standards of diversity in an effort to categorise common differences. These standards that are not intended to be an exhaustive list are:

- Race

- Age

- Gender

- Religion or Belief

- Disability

- Sexual orientation

In addition to the above 6 standards, there have been other additions including; social background, mental capability, physical capability, and other factors, which cause people to have different perspectives on the same set of facts, views and issues.

There are a series of acts covering the 6 standards of diversity. These acts were introduced to offer legal redress to any individual who feels that he / she is being discriminated against. They are:

- Race Relations Act 1976

- Sex Discrimination Act 1975

- Disability Discrimination Act 1995

- Employment Equality [Sexual Orientation] Regulations 2003

- Employment Equality[Religion or Belief] Regulations 2003

- Equality Act 2006

- Employment Equality [Age] Regulations 2006

- Gender Equality Duty 2007

Organisations that have effective diversity policies are likely to be the most risk resilient – in avoidance and mitigation – in any industrial relations issue that leads to an employment tribunal. This point is very important, because tribunal awards for cases such as sex, race and disability discrimination are on the increase, for example; around £5.2m was awarded in 2004 and in 2005 the amount awarded increased to nearly £5.6m.

TQM at Rover Group

Imported Management Techniques

Total Quality Management programmes may not always achieve an organisation's planned objectives. TQM and related Japanese or other imported management techniques, from an employee viewpoint, may be increased profits for the employer with no regards for the effects that such contributions of TQM, as a Business Process Re-engineering or change programme, may have on employees.

Total Quality Management begins with the realisation that it is relationships that organisations need to manage and there is nothing systematic about managing relationships. People always relate to others. Thus, in order to introduce TQM, it is the relationships between finance, production, marketing, research and development, and the organisation's supply chain which requires managing. Total Quality Management is about managing.

The introduction of TQM requires patience, tenacity and sustained commitment from every level of the company, starting at the top, with the CEO and the board members.

Too often, organisations in the UK see TQM as a cost rather than as a value opportunity. However, performance under TQM in some UK organisations – particularly in the motor manufacturing industry - tends to focus their attention on formalised standards and processes – like "BS" and "ISO" -, often neglecting staffing issues. In some cases companies linked individual performances and individual rewards, resulting in individuals competing against each other within the same work area, when the emphasis should be on the collective - not on individual responsibility -, for performance. TQM requires collective responsibility for company performance.

TQM, Quality Circles and JIT

By the late 1980s and early 1990s TQM and Quality Circles were being widely adopted by companies in the UK motor car industry, including "The Rover Group". Some companies – the Rover Group included – continued with earlier adopted quality systems for their supply chain, such as Just in Time (JIT) whilst introducing other systems such as TQM and Quality Circles.

The Rover Group's TQM programme incorporated its Quality Circles and JIT programmes that were introduced in the mid-1980s. However, most manufactures who in the mid-1980s were also attracted by Quality Circles and JIT programmes, suffered considerable disillusionment with those programmes and replaced them with TQM programmes, believing that TQM was the better approach to quality management through change.

By the late 1980s, due to supervisors and middle managers resistance, only about 25 quality circles covering around 150 people was in operation at the Rover Group, out of an estimated 1300 workforce. Although senior managers at Rover did not subscribe to the resistance to quality circles as the middle managers did, a high proportion felt that TQM was more successful than Quality Circles and JIT as a vehicle for the full culture change that the organisation required for its survival.

Communication at Rover

Rover introduced its TQM programme without the necessary communication and full staff consultation and this led many employees to doubt the validity of TQM and similar programmes. They argued that:

- TQM and other quality initiatives were being introduced with little regard for employee relations aspects.

- Quality issues are prioritised according to those policies and practices that are most likely to serve business rather than quality of working life objectives.

It is argued that the traditional and dominant system of control throughout UK industry is based on compliance, and although aimed at empowering workers and generate team working, still results in:

- Management by stress, where, instead of subordinating workers to direct management control, they become responsible for their own "self control".

- Giving employees additional skills, thus making them more interchangeable, they become more responsible for more aspects of their work - such as quality.

- As a result, their workloads and stress increase.

- Teams are encouraged to self-supervise and discipline their peers, thus placing new pressures on each other to perform appropriately.

- Trade unions and shop stewards become marginalised and team-leaders become the eyes and ears of management and the principal means of communication with the workforce.

Performance Monitoring

TQM at Rover seems to be based on empowerment rather than on delegation, with senior managers – to the detriment of the company - giving up authority and control to quality circle. Some organisations, on the other hand, use TQM as a tool for more centralisation and control on the other. The consequence of TQM for employees – when it is introduced in this form - is a greater intensification of work, stress and exploitation. This is emphasised by the use of electronic monitoring of worker performance.

However, with empowerment and team working, employees may take on more tasks, responsibilities and discretion – either voluntary or through peer pressure – which managers believe would increase their commitment, motivation and productivity. In such cases, employees may experience work disadvantage through:

- Work intensification and greater flexibility - working harder for no additional reward -.

- High levels of stress through additional and perhaps unwanted responsibility and new accountability.

- Social pressure from having to conform to team goals and achieve team targets and objectives.

Rover collaboration

Rover pursued the industry trend by the adoption of a number of Japanese-style production methods such as; quality circles, TQM, team-based working, and just-in-time (JIT). At Rover, this was facilitated through close collaboration with Honda, which started in 1981 with the production of the Triumph Acclaim. In 1986 the first full-time Quality Director was appointed and a form of Quality Circle was introduced soon after. However, the human resource policies and employee relations practices showed no significant changes or improvement. It appears that Honda was keen to share its production lessons/experiences with Rover but were not willing to share its experience in relation to the human dimension of their approach.

From 1990 until its purchase by BMW, Rover sought to integrate its human resources policies more tightly with its business and production strategies, although, it still had to secure the overall profitability of the business.

Rover's Training Development Programmes

By 1990, Rover had launched a programme called "Rover New Deal", which offers "no redundancies", in return for new working practices. In the early 1990s, Rover also launched a learning programme called "Rover Learning Business", which was launched with an estimated budget of over £30 million, to promote organisational learning within the group. This learning programme was expected to put Rover's emphasis on cultural change within the organisation through; training, development, teamwork and continuous improvement. The programme, however, was abandoned in 1996, after a number of senior managers who were involved in Rover's TQM programme and transformation process, left the organisation.

Rover Vulnerable in JIT Production

The main problem for the Rover Group in introducing its TQM programme and other quality management initiatives, – from my point of view – is that Rover tried to adopt Japanese style management practices into a British organisation but Japanese firms did not have the same union involvement as British firms. What is more, British firms like Rover had multiple unions involved it the car manufacturing industry. An example of this problem is the Just-in-Time production. It is argued – and I agree with the argument – that British firms in the motor industry that adopts JIT production, are very vulnerable to industrial actions that may take place anywhere in the supply chain. Rover's JIT production vulnerability was demonstrated in the following:

- The supplier of window trims and door handles for a number of Rover's makes of cars – A. J. Williams – was threatened with strike action, over a pay dispute. Senior Managers from Rover took the leading part in the talks that resolved the supplier company's dispute.

- Industrial action at Lucas Electrical – over a pay dispute - was blamed for a production stoppage at Rover. Pressure from Rover management caused Lucas Electrical to increase its pay offer that resolved the problem. Opposition to the original pay offer was the cause of the industrial action – an overtime ban -.

Human Resources Policies and TQM

It seems to me that Rover introduced its TQM programme and other quality initiatives without updating or changing its human resources and industrial relations systems and arrangements. These are very important areas of any organisation – large or small – and should be incorporated in the TQM and other quality systems. If changes to human resources and industrial relation policies are not considered as an integral part of the TQM programme and other quality systems implementation, this will show up as weakness in the organisation's management structure and procedures. Such management weaknesses would be quickly exploited by the workers.

Author's Visit to Rover

In 1992, Nottingham City Council was in the process of developing its TQM programme. The organisation was informed that The Rover Group was having some measure of success with its TQM programme, so, armed with that information, a number of Senior Managers from Nottingham City Council – including myself – arranged a one day visit to the vehicle manufacturing site of The Rover Group, to see what lessons could be learnt from Rover's TQM programme, that would be of benefit to our proposed TQM programme at Nottingham.

The visit was very useful from our point of view – Senior Managers from Nottingham City Council – because the people at Rover made us welcome and put a lot of effort into ensuring that we left their site with a good knowledge of Rover's TQM programme. However, the lessons we learnt were mainly about "Single Status" working environment, "JIT" and "Quality Circles". This we were told, was Rover's TQM programme. We concluded that Rover – for all its publicity about successfully implementing a TQM programme – had not fully implemented a TQM programme by 1992.

Quality Circles, we were told, by Rover's Finance Director, was a great idea and was working well, although you were told earlier in this book that Middle Managers at Rover were unhappy with the introduction of Quality Circles, because they lost some of their managerial authority to the Quality Circles and that made their task - managing a production line - more difficult than it would have been other-wise. The Finance Director said:

> "We had some problems with one production line; output was very low, wastage was high and that line was proving to be very inefficient. That problem was investigated by a Quality Circle consisting of ten people. They found that batches of nuts and blots did not meet the specification. Continuous monitoring of future deliveries found high percentages of nuts and bolts that did not meet the required specification, and consultation with the supplier, through letters and telephone conversations, did not rectify the problem. That Quality Circle, arranged a visit to the supplier's manufacturing site, where they spent ten

> working days, to help the supplier, find a
> solution to the problem. On there return to
> Rover, having helped to solve the problem,
> wastage on the Rover production line was
> drastically reduced and efficiency returned
> to normal."

The question I put to the Finance Director, to which I received no reply, was; when ten employees of Rover, who should have been manufacturing motor vehicles, spent ten days showing a nut and bolt manufacturer how to manufacture nuts and blots, who were manufacturing the motor vehicles? This seems to me to be a clear case of lack of managerial authority. The correspondence with the supplier should have been through the manager of the production line and if the supplier continued to fail in meeting the agreed material specification, then, change to a supplier who could produce materials to the agreed specification. If this lack of managerial authority was replicated throughout the Rover Group – and I believe it did – it is not surprising that Rover finds itself in the position of demise that it is in today.

When we looked at single status environment, the Finance Director said:

> "We are all the same in this organisation.
> We are all equal. I wear the same type of
> overall as the people on the shop-floor; I
> collected you from the reception area and
> drove the vehicle myself that transported
> you to this seminar area. I prepared the area
> and any mess made during the time you
> are here, I will tidy this area at the end of
> the day. We are proud of our single status
> working environment."

However, after providing refreshments for our group, he left the seminar area, returning fifteen minutes later to take the seminar sessions and had changed into an expensive suit for that job. One member of the group asked the Finance Director:

> "Would you pay a Driver and Cleaner salaries in excess of £90,000.00 per year? If the answer is no! Why would you pay yourself a salary in that range to do those jobs? Further, when you are driving and cleaning, who is doing the finance directing"?

Our visit to the Rover Plant was interesting, useful, educational and enjoyable. However, we concluded that Rover's approach to TQM would not be recommended to Nottingham City Council.

Total Quality Management at the Rover Group, is a typical example of a good idea not enduring the test of time. As stated in "Part One" of this book, The "Total Quality Movement" was led by a number of Quality Gurus including W. Edwards Deming, who was recruited into Japanese industry from America, to assist the Japanese with the restoration of their industry after the Second World War.

Deming embraced the Japanese industrial concept of teamwork, arguing that quality and continuous improvement requires managers to empower staff to take responsibility for the quality of their work. Rover tried to implement the Japanese style TQM - including Quality Circles -, which consists of empowering staff to work in self-managed teams, arguing that it would deliver improved quality and performance. Unfortunately, Rover did no work on changing the culture of the organisation before introducing TQM and other quality systems. Middle managers and supervisors became very unhappy because they lost command-and-control to staff empowerment and the amount of paperwork generated by TQM was taking-up too much of the time they had available. They were reduced from managers to paper-pushers.

Rover Group closed its UK motor car manufacturing business in the late 2005 with the loss of over 6,000 employees. In May 2007 Rover reopened a motor manufacturing plant in the UK with just over 200 employees – about one thirtieth of its previous workforce – under Chinese management. We await to see if; this will be a successful venture, the new management will reintroduce any of the past quality systems or TQM programme, and develop a new organisational culture since the majority of the skilled and professional employees would have gained their training and experience in the old Rover Group.

TQM in Schools

TQM is a system's approach for continuously improving the services and products that are offered to customers. In today's business and other organisation's environment, businesses and other organisations – including schools - that do not practice TQM, can become ineffective, inefficient and non-competitive very quickly. This march towards non-competitiveness can be avoided if business leaders, teachers, school managers and school governors are helped to become TQM practitioners.

Therefore, the potential benefits for schools that embrace TQM can be far reaching. For example:

- TQM can help schools provide better services to their customers – students, parents, the local community and employers -.

- The continuous improvement focus of TQM is a fundamental way of fulfilling the curriculum and financial accountability requirements of continuously changing system of educational reforms.

- Schools operating a no-fear TQM system with a focus on continuous growth and improvement, will offer more excitement and challenge to students and teachers than a "good" learning environment can provide. Therefore, the climate for learning will be improved, resulting in all-round improvement of schools, students, communities and businesses.

Schools that provide high quality teaching and learning through the implementation of a TQM programme will develop young people who:

- Are committed to the schools' ethos and values and will make those ethos and values central to their lives – both in and out of school.

- Know and understand what they are trying to achieve and what is required to get that achievement.

- Know the differences between how they have to think for each area of activity in the national curriculum.

- Have the confidence to get involved in all activities of school life, and a willingness to; demonstrate what they can do, volunteer questions and answers, take the initiative to help others, try new ideas without worrying about failing.

• Willing to take part in a range of competitive, creative and challenging activities, as individuals and as part of a team or group.

• Think about what they have to do, and make appropriate decisions for themselves, and will; work without constant prompting and direction from the teacher, ask questions that help them to organise themselves and make progress, come up with and explain a range of ideas and strategies to help them improve, react to situations intelligently.

• Show a desire to improve and achieve their potential in relation to their own abilities by; showing determination to achieve the best possible results, spend extra time preparing work and presentations, often feel that their work or performance could be better, ask for advice and information on how to improve attainment and quality of their performance.

Schools that provide high quality teaching and learning through TQM, will have high quality leadership and management to; create the schools' vision and make the vision reality. High quality leaders and managers:

• Are strategic and creative in the way that they create time, space, teachers and equipment to enable young people to learn and achieve.

- Support and develop teachers to enable young people to achieve more.

- Use the information, from monitoring and evaluating, to ensure that the school's vision is met.

- Listen to young people and act on what they say.

- Celebrate young people's achievements so that they feel successful and valued.

- Inform and involve parents/carers and listen to and act on what they say.

Such schools will also have high quality teaching to; inspire young people to learn and achieve and offer the assistance that young people need to help them learn and achieve. High quality teachers need to:

- Have a clear plan that sets out steps towards meeting the vision and expectations of their schools.

- Share with the young people, for whom they are responsible, what they are expected to achieve, in a way that they can understand.

- Take into account, what the young people have already learnt, in school as well as out of school.

- Identify the next steps, in their progression, and communicate these to the young people and their parent/carers.

- Give each pupil, relevant learning activities and authentic contexts that; interest, excite and motivate them.

- Provide opportunities for young people to; analyse, assess and evaluate their own and other student's work.

- Give young people time to; think, reflect and make decisions for themselves.

- Allow young people time to; wrestle with problems, while giving them well-timed advice and support to advance learning and avoid frustration.

- Ensure that they use; time, staff, equipment and resources in ways that keep young people interested and learning.

Since the early 1980s, schools – especially Local Education Authority (LEA) controlled schools – have been required to adapt to a vast number of changes to their internal and external environments. Having been involved with schools since the late 1970s, as a school governor, I cannot agree with the assertion that, all the Education Acts, Whitepapers and Legislations since 1980, have created the kind of improvements that favoured the customers – pupils, students and parents -. However, I feel that schools are well placed to benefit from the introduction of TQM programmes, that will help them improve and achieve; higher standards, improved teaching and learning, reduced inconsistencies across the whole education system and reduced rate of pupil disaffection.

Organisations – large or small – that have systems in place to monitor and check the standards, effectiveness and quality of services and goods being provided – schools for example -, could be more successful if a TQM programme were introduced into those organisations.

Schools have "Inspection System" that was started in September 1993. All schools were inspected, within four years of the start of the system for their type of school. After the first inspection, schools were inspected within the following six year period. Weaker schools were inspected more frequently. Schools inspection is compulsory and the period between inspections are constantly changing – a good reason for introducing TQM in schools. The schools "Inspection System" was introduced to help schools to improve, by building on the things that they do well – their strengths – and tackling problem areas, identified by them, before the inspection – their weaknesses -. Some regulations that govern school inspections are:

- The School Inspection Act 1996.

- The Education Act 1996c section 23.

- The Education (Schools Conducted by Education Associations) (Initial Articles of Government) Regulations 1993.

- The Education (Schools Conducted by Education Associations) Regulations 1993.

From the year 2000, schools in the UK have had imposed on them, a system of "Performance Management", to set standards and targets for head-teachers and their senior management teams. This system was intended to show;

what success had been achieved at the end of each cycle, any evidence that was taken into account, and the basis on which the performance was assessed, and this assessment was to form the basis for a recommendation on pay progression. There was also the intension, that this "Performance Management" system, would be rolled out to include all teaching staff, but this met with fierce resistance from a large percentage of teachers and their associated unions so, it never materialised. However, under the new Performance Management Regulations, all UK schools must have Performance Management systems in place for all teaching staff – not NQTs – by September 2007. Some of the reasons given for this imposition are:

- The 1998 Green Paper "Teachers meeting the challenge of change".

- The year 2000, introduction of Performance Management.

- Its important contribution towards raising standards.

- The new professionalism agenda.

- It strengthens the important link between school improvement and self evaluation.

Despite the above schools inspection and legislations, that are being imposed on schools; unacceptable high percentage of young people are leaving school, after 11 to 13 years full-time education, with no qualifications or with qualifications that are worthless. What is required is an education system that is fit for purpose. That is, an education system with highly committed employees, who are willing to embrace change, to ensure that through; good communication, partnerships with stakeholders – young people, parents/carers, employers, higher education institutions and local community -, and commitment to service quality with continuous improvement, the education system would be seen as a highly professional institution, that is fit for purpose and providing value for money services. A TQM programme for schools would deliver an education system that is fit for purpose and best value.

Instead of developing a TQM programme for UK schools, the Qualifications and Curriculum authority – the UK exams watchdog – have put forward new proposals for the curriculum. In those proposals, schools will be given greater freedom over how and what they teach. Such proposals, I feel, will not improve the quality of the education service provided, but will add further confusion to an already confused system.

Schools require more individual autonomy for the proposal put forward by the Qualifications and Curriculum authority – the UK exams watchdog – to be successful because schools are at different stages of development. Some schools have staff that are fully committed and who readily embrace continuous change, that leads to continuous improvement in quality of teaching and learning – for example; Roundhay School Technology College, Gledhow Lane, Leeds LS8 1ND -. However, there are other schools where, faced with the same change requirements, employees threaten industrial / strike action if those changes were implemented. In some schools, employees need a change in attitude towards continuous quality improvement through continuous organisational change before they are ready to be fully committed to the organisation. Staff commitment is not something that can be demanded, it can only be achieved through organisational culture change. Until that culture change is achieved in all schools, putting forward proposals that affects all schools equally is unlikely to be successful.

This problem occurs because, the way in which TQM and other quality systems are approached in most UK organisations – Local and Central Government and especially education – is like a writer who, half-way into his book, does not know whether it was a novel or not because the pages that had been written did not make any coherent whole.

In August 2007, Jim Knight – the Schools Minister – announced that GCSEs are robust, rigorous and respected. However, the Confederation of British industry, argued that, employers have to put on remedial English for teenagers they recruit. In addition to this, thousands of 16 year-olds are leaving school with no real competence in the subjects that matter most and employers are - rightly – expressing their concerns. Therefore, it is reasonable to argue that GCSEs are neither robust, rigorous nor respected. One employer said:

> "We are recruiting young people who have 7 and 8 GCSEs and very good IT skills but whose numeric and literacy skills are very poor. We would expect to have to train young people in IT skills but not basic numeracy and literacy."

In addition to using TQM to improve teaching and learning in general, every school and education authority should specifically equip its young people to understand the benefits that can be derived from the use of TQM to continuously improve teaching and learning. This should be a basic part of schools' contribution to readiness for work in the global economy. Whether schools' employees – teachers, support staff and managers - decide to integrate learning TQM into existing courses or to provide it as a separate course, it is important that young people <u>DO</u> and not just study about TQM.

The Development of TQM in China

TQM in China had a difficult start. The Chinese Government spent a lot of effort and money in promoting quality management, unlike Western Governments that had no involvement with the quality management concepts and its implementation in to individual organisations. The Chinese Government put polices and regulations in place, that put pressure on producers, to pay more attention to their product quality. Under such pressures from the government, the implementation rate of TQM in China became very high, especially in state-owned organisations. At the same time, because of the competition arising from China's market economy, managers took TQM in their organisations more voluntarily. Generally speaking, the senior management's commitment in improving quality is high. However, in those early years, around the late 1970s and early 1980s, the quality of products from China was still undesirable.

In that early stage of TQM development in China, there were a lot of obstacles and problems in the process of deployment of modern quality management control systems and in particular TQM in China. The following are some of the obstacles and problems faced by Chinese organisations, during their TQM implementation:

- The concept of modern quality management control systems was not properly promoted or marketed. Therefore, Chinese managers and other employees, did not have a good understanding of modern quality management principles. There were different versions of quality management concept operating in different parts of the country, and some managers were unable to distinguish between quality control and quality management.

- The approach adopted by the Chinese, in implementing their quality management systems, was top-down and caused a lot of problems. This started with the government giving directions that had the effect of forcing organisations to implement TQM. Within the organisations, the policies and regulations were also implemented from the top to the middle and bottom levels of the management before reaching the other employees. The organisations were, in effect, forcing its employees to participate, instead of encouraging them to get involved. The employees, therefore, took it as more orders from the top and they were not at all enthusiastic. This resulted in very reluctant employee participation in TQM implementation. Such authoritarian approach to quality management systems, created a lot of fears and insecurities in the workplace, which further reduced employee participation.

- The low employee participation was not only caused by the top-down approach to quality management system implementation. The Chinese society had – over the years and still is - been dominated by respect for age and hierarchy of authority. The large power distance in China made it very difficult for organisations to implement a participatory management style. Therefore, employees would rather follow orders instead of making suggestions.

- Although a lot of resources are spent on training, for managers, there is a lack of training resources, for other employees. The training provided on quality management is not comprehensive enough to reach employees at different levels within organisations. Training provided to bottom-line employees is very limited. No training is given to employees below managerial levels on; statistical control, problem solving skills and leadership skills.

- Chinese Government, developed policies and laid down regulations, for organisations to follow, on how the quality of products and services are to be improved, there was – it seems - a lack of actual government support in terms of; finance, technological support and other resources that was needed to help to drive the whole quality process. There was also, no recognition for organisations that made very good progress in raising their quality standards. The reader may say that Western organisations received no support and recognition from their respective governments for their quality programmes. However, Western governments did not involve themselves with organisational policies and did not set regulations on the quality of goods and services for organisations to follow.

- In the early quality movement Western World, it was believed - and still is - that statistical process control is one of the vital elements in improving the quality of products and services. However, in China, little emphasis was placed on statistical analysis, because organisations had limited resources and the technology in China at that time was inadequate to achieve the required statistical analysis.

- The concept of earning quick money – the get rich quick factor -, was very popular among people living in Mainland China, and that was another obstacle in improving the quality of goods and services. People would regularly sacrifice quality to achieve a higher productivity and a lower price so that they could achieve the highest profit in the shortest time.

- Because of the Chinese culture, organisations ran their business on such a friendly basis that it was very difficult for employees to treat quality systems and management seriously. Another problem occurred because; businesses contracts were awarded based on personal and family connections rather than on the quality of the products and services on offer.

Chinese Companies and TQM

Many Chinese organisations - across the full spectrum of manufacturing and commercial industries - have embraced TQM and Change Management with enthusiasm via 5-S.

The 5-S practice is a technique used to establish and maintain quality environment in an organisation. The term "5-S" stands for the following five Japanese words, developed by Osada [8]:

- Seiri, Seiton, Seiso, Seiketsu and Shitsuke.

The English equivalents, their meanings and typical examples are shown in the following table:

Japanese	English Meaning	Typical Examples
Seiri	Structurise Organisation	Throw away rubbish or return to store
Seiton	Systemise	Neatness – 30 second retrieval of document
Seiso	Sanitise	Cleaning – Individual cleaning responsibility
Seiketsu	Standardise	Standardisation – Transparency of storage
Shitsuke	Self-discipline	Discipline – Do 5-S daily

The technique has been practised in Japan for a long time. Most Japanese 5-S practitioners consider the 5-S useful not just for improving their physical environment but for improving their thinking processes as well. Apparently the 5-S can help in all walks of life. Many of the everyday problems could be solved through the adoption of this practice.

Management of Change

There is an old saying: "the only constant is change". If change is part of our daily life, how can we drive it under our control rather than being driven off by it? Change in organisation would, in the long run, lead to

change in the organisational culture. A typical example is the learning organisation, where people are excited in trying out new ideas and recognise that failure is an important part of the learning process that leads to success. Let us take a step back to look at the traditional strategic change process which can broadly be summarised by five key steps of Ho, 1999 [9]:

- Vision ==> Mission ==> Behaviour ==> Action ==> Culture

A new paradigm is:

- Action ==> Behaviour ==> Mission ==> Vision ==> Culture

The new idea here is that action leads to behaviour change of the employees. This arises from the learning process, and as Reg Raven 1983 [10] said:

> "There is no learning without action and no action without learning."

If learning is been taken successfully, the organisational behaviour will be lifted to a dynamic and challenge-seeking level. This will influence the top management in defining their mission. By achieving this, they will be confident that the mission spin off from the improved organisational behaviour, will take off as soon as it is announced.

The chief executive will then be in a position to develop the corporate vision, which should take the organisation into the realm of world class successes against all competition. Built on this firm foundation, the new vision will establish a new culture within the organisation. Being action oriented, 5-S is a powerful quality tool for everyone to get involved in the improvement process. Therefore, it is a very effective way of implementing the new management paradigm.

Is the 5-S practice applicable to the Western World? Research by Ho 1995 [11] has shown that the western world seldom recognises the significance of the 5-S practice although there are indications that some companies have included some aspects of the 5-S in their TQM programmes without being aware of its existence as a formalised quality control technique. There are many examples of successful implementation of some principles of the 5-S, especially in the service sector organisations, such as; fast-food restaurants, supermarkets, hotels, libraries, and leisure centres. The difference between the Japanese and Western approach lies mostly in the degree of employee involvement. By formalising the quality control technique, the Japanese have established the framework, which enabled them to successfully convey the message across the whole organisation, achieve total participation and systematically implement the practice. The 5-S has become the way of doing businesses – in Chinese and Japanese organisations -, not only to impress the customers but to establish effective quality processes as prerequisites for good products and services.

How 5-S is Practiced in some Organisations

The Hong Kong 5-S Campaign

In order to promote the 5-S practice in Hong Kong, its government played an important role in the massive promotional campaign that was launched and was also instrumental in facilitating an easily accessible training programme.

In 1998, the HKSAR Government approved a HK$4.6 million training programme to allow Professor Ho to train up 2,500 people within a two year period as qualified 5-S

Lead Auditors, this was the first of its kind anywhere in the world.

For the programme of training, each delegate was given a copy of the 5-S Workbook and was required to attend two half-day sessions in consecutive weekends. In between the two Saturdays, the delegates had to do the 5-S Audit of their own organisation. Ten photos had to be taken, one each for the good and bad examples of 5-S. There was a written test on the second day, and each delegate would be awarded the 5-S Lead Auditor Certificate if they pass both the live audit of their organisation and the written test. Since the launched of the programme in April 98, it is estimated that over 5,000 Lead Auditors had been trained, including a number of in-company training for the; manufacturing, service, health, education and public sectors.

In 1999, the HK 5-S Association was established and its main objective was to continue with the promotion the HK 5-S Campaign beyond the end of the funded project, which ended with the world's first 5-S Convention, held in May 99. Moreover, the training programme was franchised to the; HK Civil Service Training and development Institute, Hospital Authority, DHL, and some statutory organisations in China.

In May 2001, a questionnaire survey was conducted to establish the; suitability, importance, difficulties and benefits derived from the 5-S implementation, based on a sample size of 102 delegates who attended the Annual 5-S Convention. The findings are summarised as follows.

The suitability of the 5-S Implementation:

Most respondents found 5-S suitable for implementation at their workplace and at home. However, workshop areas find most benefit when compared with office and home.

The Importance of 5-S:

Most respondents found 5-S suitable for implementation. However, the majority people consider self-discipline to be the most important element out of the 5-S.

The hurdles in 5-S Implementation:

Most respondents found that all elements, such as; resource, time, co-operation, top management support and sub-ordinate's participation relevant hurdles which they have to overcome. Amongst these; top management support and sub-ordinates' participation they suggested are the most crucial.

The benefits of 5-S Implementation:

Most respondents found that all 10 elements were relevant benefits that they can achieve. Amongst these; safety, quality, productivity and image were the most important to them. One interesting finding was that, most of the respondents knew about; ISO 9000, ISO 14000 and OHSAS 18001, and they all agreed that 5-S is very useful as a stepping stone for their certifications.

The HK 5-S Association started issuing certificates to companies for their 5-S practice. This certification is somewhat similar to the ISO 9000 certification. The major difference is that the 5-S manual is a very thin document - not more than 50 pages, and also includes 50 standard photos -. For those who gained certified status, they found that it was very effective in motivating everyone to get involve. Hence the word "totality" of TQM. Since the HK 5-S Association launched its certification of companies in 2000, 16 companies have been registered, and many more are in the process of becoming registered. The feedback from the senior executives of the sampled companies is quoted below.

A Construction Company

> "The Hong Kong construction industry most operates under very low profit margins due to the competitive nature of the prevailing tendering systems. The hair-split difference between profit and loss is largely determined by how good our firm can organise, standardise and discipline our daily activities. We have found the 5-S useful in helping us to meet the quality and delivery requirements of our clients."

A Property Maintenance Organisation

> "5-S is a simple but effective tool, to improve productivity through, better management of the working environment. In view of the vast volume of work, as well as data, handled by the Maintenance Division, there is a need to adopt a systematic approach

to; organise information and manage our operations in order to provide a better service to public housing residents. The use of 5-S techniques provides a solid foundation for the implementation of the Quality Management System in the Maintenance Division."

A Manufacturer with Factory in China

"Neatness and tidiness have always been our principles for creating a comfortable and safe working environment for our staff. The 5-S has provided us with a framework for implementing our principles effectively and systematically."

A Retail Outlet

"We aim at producing the best traditional Chinese food, available in Hong Kong. In order to achieve this, we are totally committed to providing quality products and services to our customers. Our experience has confirmed that, the 5-S practice is a very useful tool that helps us to provide a pleasant and customer-centred environment, making eating a completely new and exciting experience."

A Government Department

"The 5-S, lays a foundation for our quality programmes, and enables us to continuously improve the services we provide to the customers. Staff can easily understand the simple and effective tools under the 5-S and apply them in their daily work with, improved results. In addition, implementation of the 5-S, provides a pleasant working environment conducive to staff morale and productivity."

The New 5-S Paradigm towards TQM

Through in-depth research in Hong Kong, Japan and the UK, Ho & Fung have identified the 5-S practice as, step number one for any organisation planning to introduce a TQM programme [Ho & Fung, 1995]. Being action oriented, 5-S is an important step towards process improvement, the key to ISO 9000, ISO 14000 and OHSAS 18001. When these quality control systems are added with; the 50-points of the 5-S element, the quality, environmental and safety management systems, that organisation is ready and can be steered towards TQM as shown in the flow diagram below:

5-S » ISO 9000 / ISO14000 / OHSAS 1800 » TQM

Since the construction industry in HK are required to be certified, in all three management systems, by their major clients, they are experimenting to see how 5-S can be used, as an integrating tool, for what is seen as a process of "Change Management". A success story coming out of HK and was recorded in one of the construction sites in Tseung Kwan O, in the Kowloon Peninsula. It has now been widely recognised as a model site for the HK construction industry, because it has; zero accident, little or no quality problems, high productivity and meeting target completion dates on all projects. However, my efforts to gain more accurate comparative data before and after changes, in order to show more significant statistical results, and analysis based on different site conditions, were not successful.

Conclusions

The 5-S practice is a well-recognised methodology used by the Japanese for improving the work environment. It was found to be a key to quality and productivity. It has been adopted and adapted to the Hong Kong business environment, through the training programme and case studies conducted by the HK Industry Department. The 5-S practice is useful because, it helps everyone in the organisation to live a better life. It is the starting point of the HK TQM programme. In fact, many successful organisations, East and West, have already included some aspects of the 5-S in their routines, without being aware of its existence as a formalised quality control technique. The Hong Kong Government is fully committed to promoting the 5-S practice in order to help its industries to improve their competitiveness. In the light of these HK TQM initiatives, I expect that the HK Company that is reopening the Rover Group will introduce a similar TQM programme at Rover, and that that initiative will create an organisational culture that will be different to what it was under the old Rover Group.

Comparison of TQM Approach

"TQM isn't a quick fix; it's a never ending programme" [1]. According to Alistair Cumming [2], TQM have made British Airways much fitter and ready for any possible competition. The process he says, "has been one of replacing negatives with positives, of doing the natural thing well, rather than the natural thing badly" [2]. He cites Gatwick Airport as an example; where British Airways employees have introduced additional lines to handle a growing workload, using existing staff and improving productivity by up to 45%.

The TQM experience at British Airways (BA) shows that the technicalities of TQM are inseparable from the basics of human relationships. In my research for this book, I found this to be the case at the; Leeds Design Consultancy, Nottingham City Council's Department of Building Works, Nottingham City Council's Contract Works, and Nottingham City Council's Design & Property Services, as well as the Rover Group.

The BA experience shows that, soft unspecific messages are no good when dealing with engineers. At the Leeds Design Consultancy, it seems to me that hard, clear proposals and practices were adopted and this seems to in line with what BA, Rover Group and Nottingham City Council did.

The BA experience shows that, TQM depends on emotions. When emotions are positive, everything becomes possible, the atmosphere gets better and attitudes will change. However, Leeds Design Consultancy, identified employees with positive emotions and the required attitudes – according to the City Architect – and those who were found lacking in the required areas, were either redeployed or offered early retirement. I felt that Senior Managers at Leeds Design Consultancy, should have spent more time in trying to change the organisation's culture through training, similar to the change programme of training carried out by Nottingham City Council's departments – Departments of; Design and Property Services, Building Works, Contract Works and Administration.

It is difficult to predict if long periods of training, or any training for that matter, will have the desired effect, because the hard-liners, for example; British Airways, British Telecom and Leeds Design Consultancy have all had some success – although limited in some cases – with their TQM programmes. On the other hand, the softly-softly organisations, for example; Westminster City Council and The Rover Group have failed to make their TQM programme successful – long term or other wise -. However, Nottingham City Council, where the organisation adopted the approach of pursuing organisational culture change – through long periods of training, for everyone in the organisation, before implementing the TQM programme – was more successful than the other organisations. Never-the-less, some members of staff at Nottingham City Council's Department of Design and Property Services have stated openly, that no amount of training could change their attitude to work and towards the organisation or even the way they do things.

Summary

The successful introduction and implementation of a TQM programme or any quality systems, into an existing organisation, requires major changes to that organisation and within that organisation. It is not realistic to suggest one systematic approach to introducing that change. There are differences in organisational and in personal styles of managing, which preclude the application of any one method. Also, the vast variation of factors present in any management situation cannot be taken into account by any single approach.

A useful guide to the influences and situations that should be considered when undertaking change programmes are as follows:

1. Recognising the need for change – this will come mainly from the manager's perceptions on:

- Weather or not there is a breakdown in effectiveness.

- Dissatisfactions expressed by his/her staff, colleagues, customers or superiors.

- The matching of what is happening within his/ her own department with what is happening elsewhere.

The search for where changes may be required can be concentrated on the following major areas:

- Structure – the reaction of staff to it. Is it too flexible or too rigid? Does it aid or hinder co-operation? Is it clear? Is there an omission or overlap of tasks?

- Tasks – can you cope with present tasks? Can you cope better with the same or different resources? Are the tasks related to your objectives? What are your objectives? Is there an omission or overlap of tasks?

- People – what are their reactions? Are their work-loads adequate? Is there effective teamwork? Are the best use being made of their skills? What are their training needs?

- Technology – is it being used effectively? Is it being used at all? Have members of staff been trained to use it? What is the impact of technology upon your staff, customers and organisational structure?

The inter-relationship between these elements needs to be considered, and the manager should aim for the best possible fit between them.

2.   Planning the Change:

- What are the objectives of the change?

- Am I dealing with the right problems, and not just the surface problems? Analyse the problem, find the solution and check other people's perception of the problem.

- What is the scope for participative discussion with staff?

- In which areas can your staff have full, partial or no say?

- Is there a deadline for achieving the change? Is the deadline flexible?

- What is the best method for accomplishing the change? How much flexibility can be introduced into the plan and the methods used?

- Is the present organisation sufficiently flexible to accept change? You may consider whether the style of managing within your organisation is mechanistic or organic, especially when planning for Quality Circles.

- Should a pilot programme be tried first? This will depend on the nature of the change. Setting up a pilot could be difficult because all stake-holders should be involved.

• Is there top management involvement? Top management should withdraw at the implementation stage but should get regular feedback.

• Can I introduce the change myself or should some other individual or groups be used as change agents?

• Have I anticipated the effects of change on other parts of the organisation? Consider the knock-on effects of the change.

• Is my programme clear, without being over-bearing?

3. Implementing the Change:

• Is the responsibility for the programme being placed at a sufficiently high level?

• How can I maintain momentum in the programme?

• Are those responsible for introducing the change acceptable to others?

• If I must devote my energy to achieving the change, have I made arrangements so that my normal work activities are not neglected?

• How can I induce commitment to the changes from others? Consider combinations from the following options; the simple provision of information, individual discussions, use of group influence, sensitivity training, the use of feedback sessions as the programme develops.

4. Checking and Monitoring the Change

- Are the effects those intended by the objectives?

- What quantitative and qualitative data can I collect?

- Does the change meet the expectations aroused in the organisation?

- Has this change highlighted the need for other changes?

Disappointment and Disillusion

Employees, whose expectations are raised, and who enjoy their new found control over their work environment, may become disappointed or disillusioned as the gains expected by management and employees fall short of those hoped for. The "What Now" phase will kick-in and senior managers have to ask themselves; how can change be sustained, and the momentum needed to achieve continuous improvement created?

The TQM package actually introduced by firms often fell short of the concepts and ideas proposed by quality gurus and the prescriptive literature. Often TQM as practiced took the form of quality circles bolted on to existing operational practice and managers who wanted "quick fixes" to problems, immediate gains and performance improvements which needed a more fundamental, penetrating approach. Senior management, anxious about middle management resistance, often limited the scope of TQM initiatives and organisational structures often did not "empower" lower-level staff to assume responsibility for quality matters.

Issues for Companies Introducing TQM

Companies or organisations pursuing TQM or any change programme will be faced with the following issues:

- Coping with continuous change – being clear about objectives, planning ahead, setting realistic targets.

- Morale & Motivation – can only be improved by explaining problems, being open to new ideas, allowing employees and customers to participate and share in developments.

- Getting the preparation right – concentrate on; service budgets, performance indicators, business plans, clients' and contractors' arrangements, training, etc.

- Improving existing services – there is a danger that existing services will be overlooked because of the pressures of new demands. The development of quality regimes, customer satisfaction surveys, performance reviews, employee involvement, and customer contracts are essential.

- The agreed programme for change should be based on; establishing a clear sense of overall purpose and direction, becoming customer driven, improving quality and performance, staff development, management development.

The evidence of this study suggests that Leeds Design Consultancy's TQM programme has had some success, particularly in the areas of cost saving, employee involvement and improved working relations. This "limited" success has positively contributed to Leeds Design Consultancy's overall change programme efforts. However, there is little evidence to indicate that there has been a noticeable change in employee attitudes. This appears to be a major drawback of the programme, although, it is probably more a reflection of the conditions that existed in Leeds City Council's Architects Department prior to reorganisation and the introduction of the TQM programme.

The unfavourable conditions into which TQM was introduced, do not appear to have been more or less detrimental to the programme's success, than the favourable conditions cited for BA and BT. Never-the-less, one is left with the feeling that a management style that is both supportive and attentive, will generate a more positive perception of management and therefore, encourage greater employee acceptance and greater employee involvement. Arguably, an organisation with this type of management style does not need TQM, and this may be true, unless TQM is looked at from a different point of view.

There is a place for TQM in Local Authority Organisations or any company where the need to provide high quality services is essential. Invariably, such organisations already have a strong quality control tradition. This tradition complements a concept that has produced its biggest paybacks in solving quality related problems, and where workers have traditional professional skills.

However, local authority organisations, manufacturing companies and other service organisations that do not have a strong quality control tradition, must not feel that they could never benefit from TQM. Some benefits will accrue for organisations in this second category, and I feel that these organisations will benefit far more than those that already have strong quality control tradition. Managers in such organisations should therefore, refrain from under-selling the concept, and adopt a more long-term approach. In such cases, the TQM concept must be viewed as a long-term measure towards a broader programme of involvement.

Managers need to put more effort into making their staff feel more comfortable or positive about TQM or any other quality systems. The following ideas may be helpful:

1. Identify and understand the needs and personal goals of your staff. Beware of your assumptions, which may be false and misleading.

2. Remember that money is not the only motivator. There are many other rewards that could be used, to influence staff, more effectively than money. Money alone is not always effective in getting employees' commitment.

3. Set your staff targets which are realistic and achievable but would also stretch ability. If possible, involve staff in setting their own targets.

4. Always recognise achievement by praise or some other award.

5. Do not alter targets without consulting with the staff concerned. If changes are necessary, these should be agreed jointly.

6. Harness the strength of the group. Group pressures can affect staff attitudes to work, positively as well as negatively. Involving your staff as a group in making decisions, will strengthen commitment.

7. Keep your staff informed about what is going on in the whole organisation.

8. It is what people expect to get out of the work they do that motivates them to behave in particular ways. An effective manager is one who creates conditions, which enable individuals to reach their personal goals through achieving the goals of the organisation.

9. Information about aspects of the organisation's operation, and how it relates to the company's financial position, should be made readily available to employees and their representatives. In many organisations, although they have structured arrangements for handling information or consulting with employees about company plans and progress – including joint union and management committees – there are still many problems caused by the methods of communication, and restrictions on disclosure at joint committee and employees meetings.

10. Employee participation in change, will help overcome resistance to change, and promote faster re-learning of new methods, higher efficiency, and

reduced hostility, since employees will feel that the changes were within their control.

11. Those who might resist change should be involved in planning and implementing it. Collaboration can have the effect of reducing opposition and encouraging commitment. It helps to reduce fears that individuals may have about the impact of changes on them and makes use of individuals' skills and knowledge.

12. Managers should share their knowledge, perceptions and objectives with employees, especially those who will be affected by change. This may involve; training programme, face to face counselling, reports, memos, and group meetings and discussions. Employees may need training so that they can recognise the problems that necessitate change. It is therefore, necessary, to get the facts straight and to discuss and reconcile opposing points of view. To do this, managers need to trust their employees and management must appear credible to their employees.

13. Employees should be given counselling and therapy, to help overcome their fears and anxieties about change. It may be necessary to develop individual awareness of the need for change, as well as the individual's self-awareness of feelings towards change and how these feelings could be altered.

14. Management should negotiate rather than impose change, where there are individuals or groups who will be affected and who have enough power to resist. Some managers feel that this will create

a precedent for future changes, which may also have to be negotiated although the circumstances surrounding them may be quite different. This is not necessary, so management's fears and anxieties may be overcome if the education and communication, outlined in 12 above are met.

15. The workforce is the biggest single resource without whose involvement and commitment, services cannot be improved. Therefore, the over-riding emphasis of organisations' management should be on communication. Without good communications success is impossible. Good communication is not the same as good directions and a dialogue must be developed with all employees whereby they have a full opportunity to contribute ideas, question policies and practices and respond to change. The workforce should be valued. Like customers, they are much closer to the problems.

16. It is important to raise staff awareness of the potential conflicts that may arise. Employees need to explore prejudices and assumptions that will exist between teams as well as between departments. Employees need the opportunity to voice their fears and talk about changes together, as a team.

Some personal goals include:

• A need to feel a sense of achievement.

• Recognition for good work.

• Advancement and promotion.

- Participation in decision making.

- Increased responsibility.

- Freedom to plan and organise own work.

- Challenge and personal development.

However, it is important to accept that people are motivated in different ways. It is therefore, not possible to provide specific solutions to the problems of changing attitudes and motivation. These differences must be recognised and should form the basis of any approach you use in attempting to understand and influence the attitude to work, of your staff.

The Recipe

There is no doubt that the implementation stage of any TQM programme is crucial. However, the ground rules for successful implementation are well tried and established, so it is difficult to come up with anything new. Never-the-less, organisations are continuing to introduce the TQM concept into British organisations and failing, in spite of having a well tried and established formula. With the over-emphasis on implementation, it is quite easy to put failure down to the omission of some key ingredient, but if the key conditions necessary for successful implementation can never be absolutely achieved, what chance is there of success? Is this a failure on the part of the organisations, to follow the formula, or a convenient excuse for dedicated followers of the concept, to use when TQM programmes fail?

These are difficult questions to answer on the basis of my study. Leeds Design Consultancy's implementation strategy was deficient on a number of crucial points, and would have benefited from a pilot study approach. But more significantly, a lack of organisational support from the lower echelons is a reflection, more on the prevailing attitudes within the organisation than on the TQM programme. My experience of the Leeds Design Consultancy's programme suggests that upward push from first-line managers that is so essential for TQM to succeed is probably the most difficult element to reproduce when translating the concept. This lack of upward push, together with lower standards of education at first-line management level, are the likely cause that lead to the narrow range of projects tackled and the lack of innovation. This problem is typical of most local authority organisations.

Does this mean that there is no guarantee of success, no matter what recipe for introducing TQM is applied? My feelings are that many organisations, that are introducing TQM and other quality programmes, are overlooking the long baking time – continuing my analogy of a recipe – and expecting the cake to rise by turning up the heat.

TQM demand a whole new management style that does not exist in many local authority and public sector organisations at this point in time. To develop the necessary management style requires the gradual implementation of a whole range of management techniques, so that changes in perceptions and attitudes can be facilitated. This process cannot be rushed, but it must be implemented with determination. Using a drip-feed approach, every effort must be made to break down traditional "us and them" attitudes. In some cases, this may lead ultimately to the Japanese style "single status" organisation. However, senior managers, in British organisations, will have to be mindful that the culture of their organisation is such that it may not be ready for "single status" operation; otherwise – as with the Rover Group –

managers may find that they lose their authority for making managerial decisions. Managers still have a responsibility to manage and lead their organisations, even in "single status" operations.

The "Greenfield site", like the "Nissan" plant, located in the North West of England, was obviously a fertile ground where new concepts were able to flourish. Because the area had very high unemployment and people had to be retrained for the new industry, it was easy to incorporate into the training, the required organisational culture as part of that training package.

A large number of departments, in local authority organisations – social services, education, housing, etc. – are perusing various quality accreditations, and voluntary organisations are following suit. However, I have yet to come across a quality accreditation that has customer satisfaction and or organisation efficiency as the driving force or featuring high in the priorities set, in senior managers' decision making process.

If public and voluntary organisations are to introduce TQM programmes successfully, they must:

- Identify and embrace the positive aspects of their continuously changing environment.

- Change and improve organisations' results by changing organisations' culture and staff behaviour.

- Adopt an integral approach to organisational and individual development.

- Recognise the impact of change on people and address how they can be appropriately supported, by the organisation and its leadership.

- Monitor performance continuously – not just when preparing for audit – so that the services provided, can continue to improve.

- Use information gained through feedback to shape and improve the way resources are allocated. This feedback can be both qualitative and quantitative and can be in the form of; surveys, compliments and complaints and may be from sources such as; employees, customers, partners, clients and other stakeholders.

- Use performance indicators with simple measures that tell you how the organisation is doing. These can be compared with previous performance and benchmarked against the performance of similar organisations, to tell you where you are doing well, and where you need to do better. These can be measures of cost, quality or timeliness.

- Use external reviews and inspections by inspectorates and regulators established by the Government, to provide an impartial view of how your company is performing and how the organisation is tackling the challenges that it faces.

- Monitor progress against a plan of key elements and have a performance management and reporting system in place, to ensure that there is full accountability, for achieving set targets.

- Focus management action on your highest priority areas, but ensure that that performance improves across the whole organisation, through the implementation of a "Best Value Performance Plan".

Taking Leeds City Council as an example:

The City Council, it seems, have learnt no lessons from the experience of Leeds Design Consultancy. In a number of cases, sections within a single department, would apply for quality accreditations just because they – the managers of those sections – assume that it looks impressive on their sections' letter-heads. Some managers argue that it gives them an advantage over others when applying for funding or competing for funds for the provision of certain services.

Some City Council Departments have spent periods of one year to 18 months on departmental restructuring, and only after such restructuring, are the senior managers of those departments, introduced to the principles of quality systems. Some of these quality systems are being miss-sold by unscrupulous consultants, who set themselves up as "quality experts", and are able to sell, worthless quality systems, to unsuspecting managers, who have no knowledge of quality systems, and who had not taken the time to do the necessary reading before employing consultants.

As the Quality Manager of Nottingham City Council Building Works said:

> "We had to read a lot and we had to learn fast but it still took us 18 months to set up the system. We employed consultants as advisers. They were helpful but very

expensive because they charged on a day rate visit basis but they did not give us any information unless we asked for it. What made it so expensive, was the fact that we did not know what we required, so we did not know what questions to ask, and if we did not ask the question, we did not get the information. As soon as we were able to struggle through on our own, we did not have the consultants in.

You must have all staff support, which is most important. Without the support of all staff, including senior managers, we would have failed. We sold it to staff as their system, it is owned by each section and each individual, so everyone gave it their full commitment, because no one wants it to be said that he or she let the side down".

And The Assistant Quality Manager of Nottingham City Council Building Works said:

"We have a system in place, we have "published procedures" and everyone is doing their best to make it work, but there are still problems. People are expected to look at the way they do things and to come up with ideas to modify the procedures, but some people are not reporting the modifications and this is just as costly if not more costly than keeping the old procedures. We overcame this problem, by setting up our own Quality Auditors, to undertake quality audits. The training for this was very expensive because it meant training a lot of people. The Quality Auditors go into other sections and carry out quality audits on that section; we then use the information from the audit to update our operations procedures centrally. A Quality Auditor cannot audit his own section. We have two people in each section quality audit trained.

We are quite happy with it now but it was not easy. We had to put a lot of work into it, but now we have operations procedures for each section, both in folders and on computer. Having the procedures on computer is good because some sections have overlapping procedures, so if one section changes one of its procedures, the computer will identify all sections with a similar procedure and update their operating procedures. Just in case people go for some time without checking for procedural changes on their computer, a paper memo is sent - automatically – to all sections that will be affected by the changes.

We are coping well with changes, and managing the operations are so much simpler now, because everyone feel that they have a responsibility, not just to making the systems work, but to look for ways of improving the systems and assist with the implementation of those improvements. However, this also caused some problems because, people were so enthusiastic about

> implementing improvements, and they
> were sometimes implemented without the
> necessary communication and feedback.
> This was where the Quality Auditors came
> into their own, by picking up those changes
> and making sure that they are fed back to
> the centre and communicated to everyone
> who will be affected".

Evidence however, suggests that TQM can succeed, where organisations have a well-established tradition of providing quality goods and services, for example; British Airways' Technical Workshops, Barnsley City Council and Nottingham City Council. Organisations – service or manufacturing – must strive to attain new quality bases, by raising the educational standards of the whole workforce. A tall order you may say, but it is not impossible. Statistical methodology, which is so very important in any organisation's TQM activities, may already exist in a quality conscious organisation. For such organisations, transferring those techniques and applying them to solve TQM problems would be much easier than for organisations with no tradition of quality.

Is the introduction of a TQM programme worth all this organisational effort? I believe it is. If TQM is no longer regarded as a stand alone technique, then its implementation should be regarded as a measure of how progressive an organisation is, and is far removed from traditional industrial relations that is based on conflict.

TQM Implementation Phases

TQM programme should be planed so that it follows a set of steps or phases. Set out below are recommended phases for a successful TQM.

Phase One – The Preparation:

> This step establishes the internal support and the understanding within the organisation. It will attempt to convince all employees – including managers – of the value of TQM and establish the funds to support the programme. Based on an agreed criteria; appropriate programmes of visits, readings, discussions, budget co-ordination meetings and training programmes should be selected.

Phase Two – Networking of Stakeholders:

> This step establish a network of all interested or affected agencies, including employees as well as senior managers and those at policy making levels. At this stage, the budget should be established and made available. Teams to facilitate implementation and co-ordination should also be established and trained.

Phase Three – TQM Concepts and Tools Introduced:

> This step should provide the basic understanding – for all employees – of the TQM concepts and tools. The understanding

of such tools should be tested in a classroom setting and a follow-up plan should be arranged.

Phase Four – Training:

This step should start giving staff the basic understanding of Total Quality Management, especially those at managerial and supervisor levels. It should enthuse employees to start activities that would develop basic TQM skills and also build support and commitment.

Phase Five – TQM Testing:

This step should test the proposed TQM in the working environment, to show to what extent the concepts can be used, to analyse and solve problems. It should also develop activities and programmes that would address; organisational needs, documentation of activities, creation of a learning environment, informal training and build support and commitment.

Phase Six – Quality Teams Established:

Quality teams – not to be confused with quality circles – should be responsible for the management, coordination and the monitoring of the TQM programme. The quality teams should also ensure; that plans of actions and implementation of activities are developed, that programme of activities are defined and communicated and that such activities are appropriately implemented.

Phase Seven – Monitoring and Evaluation:

This step will draw conclusions about the TQM processes and procedures that would allow adjustments to be made to the approaches used in introducing the associated processes. Monitoring and evaluation activities should involve all stakeholders and successes and lessons learnt, recorded and used in continuous improvement of products and services.

Strategy for Successful TQM

For TQM to be successful, organisations will have to meet the requirements set out in the "TQM Requirements Table."

Successful TQM Requirements	Organisational Culture Requirements
A systematic way to improve products and services.	Customer satisfaction by listening to their requirements.
Long term plans for organisational development.	Identify the cost of providing quality products and services.
Identifying and solving problems through a structured approach.	"Doing things right first time every time."

Actions needed are conveyed by management.	Everyone at all levels in the organisation taking ownership for their actions.
Statistical quality control is used as a supporting function.	Have systems in place for continuous process improvement.
Everyone is pursuing the same goals.	Top managers demonstrating strategic leadership.

If the organisation meets the requirements set out in the "Requirements Table", the following outcome may result:

- Rewards and recognition for staff at all levels.

- Top management support and direction.

- The organisation will have full commitment to training.

- There will be a focus on customer needs.

- Effective communications throughout the organisation.

- A reliance on standards and measures.

- Employees would be involved and feel empowered.

- The commitment will be long-term.

For the successful implementation of a TQM programme, organisations require the following:

- Organisations should put more effort into identifying reasons for employees' resistance to total quality management (TQM) and try and reduce any fears that may lead to such resistance. One of these fears may be that employees feel that the TQM programme is a controlling mechanism rather than one of empowering the workforce. Another factor is that workers may see TQM as a ploy to get them to increase productivity for no additional rewards. In some organisations, TQM may be seen as empowering but not all individuals in that organisation ore motivated by empowerment. In fact some people do not want empowered jobs. Resistance to TQM programmes are not always related to perceptions that organisations seeking products and services improvements through TQM are seen as controlling. In such cases resistance is due to personality characteristics, organizational culture and individual's behaviour within the organisation's quality environment.

- Organisations that are implementing TQM or any other quality programmes have to work hard at reducing or illuminating barriers to those programmes. The barriers may include; reluctance to any type of change on the part of the workforce, employees may lack any form of identification with the quality control initiatives, and the size of the organisation. Important factors that will help to reduce these barriers and lead to success include; active support from the top – the CEO -, create awareness and acceptance for the TQM programme by continuous publicity - internal as well as external -, staff development training aimed at changing the organisational culture, and an appropriate

R. *Ashley Rawlins TD. DL.*

reward system linked to incentive schemes. The organisation should integrate all quality control systems and any other team type initiatives that strive for continuous improvement into the TQM programme. Organisations tend place greater emphasis on quality control systems and statistical methods but at the same time neglecting customer satisfaction and quality assurance. However, quality management based on internal quality control systems is a long way off Total Quality Management –TQM -.

- The commitment to creating enduring value by focusing on efficiency in everything that they do. Their goal should be to deliver constantly good results by out performing all regulatory and financial targets and delivering efficiency across the whole organisation. This could be achieved by sharing best practise and employing the best affordable technology that is available.

- They should aim to provide a quality of service that is significantly better than any other and at a price that represents good value for money. To do this, they will have to design their services from the outside-in, considering the customers' point of view and eliminating service failures. This will lead to improved operational performance and an enjoyable customer experience.

- Organisations Quality Management System (QMS) should be a set of policies, processes and procedures used specifically for the purpose of planning and execution of production, development and service in their core business area of the Organization.

QMS should integrate the various internal processes within the organization and provide a process approach for the execution of all activities. Through QMS the organization should be able to identify measure, control and improve the all areas of its business processes and that will lead ultimately to improved business performance.

- Organisations should aim to create a great place for its people to work in, with zero accidents, a good work-life balance and the opportunity to make a real difference. This would help organisations to attract and retain the best people, with performance and contribution recognised. Success should be rewarded and celebrated as part of the organisation's culture.

- Organisations should aim to achieve 100% compliance with all legal and regulatory obligations and to go beyond compliance where the benefits exceed the cost.

- Organisations should aim to make a positive difference to society. This could be achieved by actively involve their people in community volunteering and external leadership roles and influencing matters relating to their business.

- Organisations should create a new level of partnership, understanding and transparency with all customers, clients and key service providers. The aim here is to achieve win-win-win positions, which provide better customer service, lower costs and ever increasing efficiency. To make this happen, organisations must set clear expectations and encourage new ideas and innovation.

Is TQM Still Relevant in 2007 & Beyond?

According to Regina Kay Brough [12], "TQM is a set of Principles, Tools and Procedures that provide guidance in managing and achieving organisational goals and objectives. TQM is about results. It involves everyone in continuously improving how work is done to meet customer expectations of quality. And through interactions, the process improves. And, finally and importantly, TQM is an attitude."

Organisations that embrace TQM will be able to use those techniques to explore the problems they face and find appropriate solutions with positive response from their people and customers. Top managers in those organisations will be able to look at the behaviour of their organisations, departments, teams and individuals to identify the necessary changes that will support the achievement of sustained improvements.

In 2007 top executives and senior managers are making statements such as:

- Senior Manager - BT

  "As a reasonable company, we strive for continuous improvement and work to a strong set of values which ensure everyone who deals with us is treated fairly."

- Board Member – Building Society

"I want our customers to feel assured that they are part of our growing and successful organisation in which they can remain confident, both now and in the future."

- Senior Manager - Manufacturing

"We have a team of committed and dedicated people who believe in the values of the organisation and support the communities. They have worked extremely hard to deliver quality products and services over the past year, and we are truly grateful".

Public Sector TQM

Since the late 1990s, public sector organisations have been showing increased interest in TQM and it is argued that the reasons for such increased attention being given to the implementation of TQM is that TQM:

o Taps the expertise of front-line staff.
o Encourages employees to be innovative.
o Productivity gains are achieved.
o Jobs are enriched.
o Teamwork is promoted.
o Internal and external communication improves.
o Employees develop leadership skills.
o Creates an effective response to communities' demand for better service from all departments, including government.

- Director – Local Authority Organisation

"We continue to demonstrate the successful application of a diverse strategy, delivering consistently improving services. We believe in our future and in our ability to grow and prosper. We have very capable and passionate people who have achieved a great deal and through them we continue to deliver outstanding quality services."

- Chief Executive – Computer Services Provider

"We have innovative people, quality products and services and we are growing our customer base. Our diversity strategy helps us to maximise efficiency and this in turn enables us to invest for the long term and ensure continuing benefits for all."

- Managing Director – Engineering Services

"Listening to our customers and staff and seeking their views on our products and services is a vital component in our drive for continuous improvement. This is in line with our aspiration to provide exemplary quality service to our customers."

A major challenge faced by local authority organisations and government departments that may be interested in TQM is finding the funds needed to get it started. Budget limitations may cause many of these organisations to start their TQM implementation very slowly. They have to seek funds through grants, or special funds from local foundations, or from large corporations who are willing to form "partnerships" with local authorities and government departments for little or no financial gain.

One way for such organisations to find the funds needed, is to start with a pilot TQM programme and select an area for that effort that will produce – with some certainty – large budget savings or increased revenue. The savings from the first TQM project may then be utilised to support the second and third, and so no until the TQM programme is established throughout the whole organisation.

The British Airways actions after the launch of its TQM are not recommended. BA ran a pilot TQM programme, which saw a turn round of its Technical Workshops. However, BA took the short-term option and rather than using the success and profits gained from this pilot TQM to fund and support TQM in other areas of the organisation, BA sold that successful arm to make quick profit. Organisations should remember – during their planning for TQM - that TQM programmes are "long-term" projects.

- Chief Executive – Local Authority Organisation

  "Our people are at the heart of our corporate agenda. We rely upon their commitment, professionalism, and expertise in delivering customer service excellence. We provide ongoing investment to their learning and development to achieve the highest standards, recognised through our investor in people status since 1998. Opportunities for employment, career progression and development, irrespective of gender, ethnic origin, age, religion or disability, are fully supported and enabled through our Equal

Opportunities policy and Positive about Disabled People status."

• A Director and Board Member – NHS Trust

"We use a range of effective two-way communication methods to ensure our people and their representatives are informed about, and engaged with our strategic direction. These include face-to-face presentations and briefings by senior management, people surveys, the intranet, our Connections team briefing process, our breakfast seminars and change forums outlining progress on key projects. The positive impact of our status as a responsible employer continues to be borne out by low levels of staff absence for our sector. Regular consultation with our Staff Association ensures that our people's views on the services we provide are fully and objectively represented."

Organisations today are seeking to deliver more integrated services and hence require new ways of working. If better quality services and products are to be achieved, they will require a change in the work culture of the organisation. This will not be easy for a workforce that is accustomed to working within narrow professional boundaries. For companies to achieve continued improvement, especially organisations that are made up of multi-disciplinary departments and teams of professionals, they must develop better and more effective communications across departs and professional boundaries. One way to achieve this is to co-locate managers from different services to work together in multi-disciplinary teams. This working model will give professionals from different services day-to-day contact and this will result in better co-operation between professionals. This in turn will result in continued improvements in quality and efficiency. Such teams, however, will need to ensure effective day-to-day leadership as well as professional supervision and guidance.

Some organisations – be they large or small – that talks a lot about quality systems but do little else, do so at their peril, for example; in July 2007, BAA, the airport operator ask its regulator, the Civil Aviation Authority, to consider suspending a penalty clause relating to service quality. The clause requires BAA to pay rebates to airlines if the airport fails to meet certain quality standards. Senior managers at BAA should take a lesson from the Chief Executive of a Third Sector Organisation who reported the following at his board meeting:

> "We have now completed the training on Quality Improvement Systems for all our employees. Their assignments have been submitted and we are awaiting their results and accreditation. I have also completed the advanced skills section for managers as well as our Self-Assessment Report (SAR). I am now in the process of completing the full manual, which will help us put together a detailed plan for the development and implementation of a quality improvement framework."

UK Quality Training Initiatives

In the millennium – more than in any other era – organisations are talking about; quality costs, managing change, quality circles, quality commitment, leadership and management systems framework, integration and business management related standards, improvement planning through tools, quality benchmarking, strategic supply chain management, quality of service provision, quality audits, quality improvement teams, quality councils, quality statements, just-in-time (JIT), quality revolution, TQM and the need to meet the requirements new quality standards and certifications such as:

- o   ISO 9001:2000
- o   BS EN ISO 1400
- o   ISO 9000
- o   BS 5750
- o   Quality Network
- o   Quality Assurance
- o   Excellence Awards for Quality
- o   Investor in People
- o   Quality Systems Audit
- o   Quality Management Tools
- o   Quality Systems Assessment

In the UK, financial assistance for quality systems and quality audit training, including TQM are now available to Organisations, through various government-backed initiatives, and I give some examples below:

- •   Training funded by Business Links (Small Business Services) and the T.E.C.

- Invest in Skills and Train2Gain – both these programmes have been promoted through the "Come and Get It" Campaign (www.20m4u.co.uk).

- Invest in Skills offer up to 40% of the direct cost of training and is funded by the Learning and Skills Council (South Yorkshire), Objective 1 European Social Fund (ESF) and Yorkshire Forward (SRB6).

- Training2Gain offer up to 100% training discount and wage replacement and is run by Learning and Skills Council (South Yorkshire).

- For manufacturing companies in the West Yorkshire region, the Best Practice Skills Transfer Programme, administered by Yorkshire Company Services, provides up to 65% grant funding.

- Similar arrangements operate in other areas of the UK.

Quality control activities were predominant in the 1940s, and it continued to grow until the 1970s when an era of quality engineering took hold and by the late 1970s, when top managers were expected to get involved and drive the systems rather than leaving it to the engineering professionals. This saw the introduction of several quality systems that were management led and finally the introduction in the UK of TQM, which was an integration of the various quality systems. From the 1990s we have seen such a rapid increase in TQM and other quality systems as an emerging specialist Professional field. In the millennium, like medicine, accounting, and engineering, quality has achieved status as a recognized profession. TQM and other quality systems will continue well beyond the millennium and there will soon be a time – in the UK at least – when organisations will not be awarded contracts unless they have TQM or some other quality systems in place and able to prove that it is not just a paper exercise.

TQM is very much alive in today's business environment – including service organisations – and will continue into the future of successful organisations because TQM is about how organisations:

- Identify the needs and requirements of customers and employees.

- Provide goods and services that satisfy the needs and requirements of customers.

- Develop organisations' cultures that satisfy the development and career needs of employees.

- Implement management / quality systems to monitor and modify the above to ensure best available output of goods and services.

- Manage and maintain the management / quality system so that monitoring and modifications become a continuous process in the organisation.

References

1. David Ellis: "D T I 90s News", October 1992.

2. Cumming: "How BA Engineered Its Turnaround". Management Today, September 1992.

3. Henry Mintzberg & James Quinn: "The Strategy Process, Concepts, Contexts, Cases"; Second Edition, pp 345. Prentice-Hall, International Edition.

4. Henry Mintzberg & James Quinn: "The Strategy Process, Concepts, Contexts, Cases" Second Edition, pp 345. Prentice-Hall, International Edition.

5. Henry Mintzberg & James Quinn: "The Strategy Process, Concepts, Contexts, Cases"; Second Edition, pp 346. Prentice-Hall, International Edition.

6. R. Ashley Rawlins: "The Millennium Manager"; Author-House Publications, 2006.

7. Erika Lucas: "Making Inclusion a Reality"; Professional Manager, Volume 16, July 2007.

8. T. Osada: The 5-S; Five Keys to a T.Q. Environment, Asian Productivity Organisation, Tokyo 1991.

9. S.K.M. Ho: TQM; "An Integrated Approach, Implementing TQ through Japanese 5-S and ISO 9000", Kogan Page, UK 1995 & 1997 Ed., HKBU 1999 Ed.

10. Reg Revans: "ABC of Action Learning"; Chartwell-Bratt, UK 1983.

11. S.K.M. Ho & C. Fung: "Developing a TQM Excellence Model – Part 2"; TQM Magazine, MCB Volume 7, No. 1, UK, February 1995.

12. Regina Kay Brough: "The Eight Rules for   Producing Results"; The Journal of State Government, January – March 1992, pp4..

ABOUT THE AUTHOR

Major R. Ashley Rawlins TD DL BA
DMS MSc MBA MCMI

Major Ashley Rawlins a Nevisian, born in Rawlins Village, Gingerland, Nevis, West Indies to William and Veronica Rawlins, moved to Matchman's Road, Gingerland, Nevis at age 8 years. The first of four children; Mrs. Ullida Gill, Hon. Mr. Justice Hugh Rawlins and Mr. Franklyn Rawlins. Grew up in Gingerland, attended The Gingerland Senior School and the Gingerland Methodist Church before moving to the UK as a teenager.

Design Engineer, Energy Manager and Project Leader, British Telecom Plc. Senior Design Manager, Leeds City Council. Senior Manager, Utilities and Energy Management, Nottingham City Council. Contracts Manager, EnviroEnergy Ltd, one of Europe's largest combined heat and power schemes. Part-time Lecturer in Building Services Engineering. Member of Governing Body for two high schools and one primary school and chair of one high school governing body. Director and Board Member of UCA House. Director, Chair and Board Member of Leeds Interpreting and Translation Services Ltd. Director and Board Member of Chapeltown and Harehills Enterprise Ltd. Director, Chair and Trustee of Leeds Chapeltown Citizen's Advice Bureau. Member of the Institute of Electrical and Electronics Incorporated Engineers, member of the interviewing panel and interviewed applicants for membership in the North East and Midlands from 1988 to 1992. Member of the East Midlands Energy Management Group, the Nottingham Green Partnership Energy Group, the Nottinghamshire Environmental Topic Forum and Chaired the Nottingham City Council's Energy Conservation Group. Chair of Ardsley and Robin Hood BLP. President of Morley RBL. Member of Sheffield Business School's Change Management Forum during its early stages. Member of the Chartered Management Institute. Appointed Her Majesty's Deputy Lord-Lieutenant for the County of West Yorkshire. Author of Book – "The Millennium Manager", published by Author House, February 2006.

Printed in the United States
148251LV00001B/7/P